MW00918129

"And I saw three unclean spirits like frogs

come out of the mouth of the dragon,

and out of the mouth of the beast,

and out of the mouth of the false prophet.

For they are the spirits of devils,

working miracles,

which go forth unto the kings of the

earth and of the whole world,

to gather them to the battle

of that great day of God Almighty."

REV 16:13-14

THE FALSE PROPHET

ELLIS H. SKOLFIELD

*"Truth can never be told
so as to be understood
and not be believed."*

WILLIAM BLAKE

FISH HOUSE PUBLISHING

Copyright 2001

All rights reserved. No part of this book may be
reproduced in any form or by any electronic or
mechanical means including information storage and
retrieval systems without specific permission in
writing from the publisher except by a reviewer
who may quote brief passages in review.

Except where noted, Bible quotations are from
the King James Bible. A few are from the
New American Standard version
The Lockman Foundation
1960, 1962, 1963, 1968, 1972, 1975, 1975, 1977
and are quoted by permission.
One quotation is from the NIV.
Three are from Green's Interlinear Bible.
Extensive quotes from Islam Reviewed
are by permission.

This book in its entirety,
including graphs and illustrations,
was generated in Corel Word Perfect 10

ISBN 0-9628139-6-6

FISH HOUSE PUBLISHING

P.O. Box 453
Fort Myers, Florida, 33902

Printed in the United States of America

PUBLISHER'S NOTE

THIRTY years ago all notable prophecy teachers pronounced, as if from on high, that the USSR was the final satanic end-time empire of all time. A laughable concept now, long abandoned. However, other fanciful views still cloud men's minds and flood our bookstores – imaginations for which there is little scriptural support. These "traditions of men" are immensely popular and why shouldn't they be? Doesn't everyone want to hear a tranquilizing song, true or not, that lulls us into believing we will be spared a time of trouble? Of course. So despite the ever-worsening Islamic terrorist attacks upon our people, with Armageddon looming on the horizon, will the church have ears to hear this "wake-up call from hell," as Israel's Binyamin Netanyahu termed New York's smoking ruins?

Beginning in 1979 with a *Revelation Chart* and a little book called *Daniel is Out of Chronological Order* (both now out of print), Skolfield's books on Bible prophecy have become standard reference works for prophecy students of many denominations. From the beginning of his ministry, Skolfield taught that the final empire to come against the Church and Israel would not be the communist world or a "New World Order," but Iraq, Iran, Syria, and the radical Moslem fundamentalists of the Middle East. And so it has proven to be.

Much of this new book will be familiar to those who have read *Sozo* or the *Hidden Beast* series. However, there is much here that is new. Additional subjects needed to be addressed or illustrated. Of necessity, there are still chapters on the "Time of the Gentiles," day=years, time-times, and so on. Please forgive the repetition, but those not familiar with the prophetic principals spelled out in the author's earlier works would be totally lost if those concepts were not included.

Thnks all so go to Tabi an Jan, too vare pashunt Inglish teechurs who kep the authur frum lookin like a totul ideut.

v

Contents

viii

List of Illustrations

Dedication

They were stoned,
they were sawn asunder,
were slain with the sword:
they wandered about in sheepskins
and goatskins;
being destitute, afflicted, tormented;
of whom the world was not worthy:
they wandered in deserts,
and in mountains,
and in dens and caves of the earth.

HEB 11:37-38

IT began with Stephen, saints dying for Jesus: stretched on the rack, boiled in oil, cast in among serpents, thrown to lions. Four to twenty million killed by the Roman Empire, and thirty million since: skinned alive, burned at the stake, babies dashed against walls, pregnant women ripped open. Millions murdered by Nazis, a million Sudanese butchered by Moslems – many by crucifixion. In Cambodia, a million more, and Christians in Nigeria, too. Those brethren, gone to the Lord before us, stand beneath the altar and never cease to cry: "How long, O Lord, holy and true, dost thou not judge and avenge our blood on them that dwell on the earth?" (Rev 6:10)

This unworthy work is dedicated to those precious tribulation saints and to the brethren who have yet to face their murderers in some dank and rat-infested dungeon. And it is to you, my beloved brother or sister in the Lord, for as sure as night follows day, that same fate awaits many who will read this book.

Preface

OUT of the deserts of the Middle East he came, a false prophet, and out of that same Euphrates Valley came his followers, the final foes of the Church and Israel. "Three unclean spirits like frogs" is what the Bible calls them. They are the international Islamic terrorist organizations and militant Islamic states of Iraq, Iran and Syria who fund and protect them. These three Middle Eastern countries and their associates are the Leopard-Bear-Lion beast of Revelation, and the malevolent influence of that devilish trident can be felt over the whole world as "they gather the kings of the earth together for the battle of the great day of God Almighty."

Arutz Sheva Israel National Radio, 9/30/2001, 4:43pm
by Moshe Feiglin

I came to the US for four days, for a meeting that was to have been held in Manhattan on Tuesday evening, September 11. The meeting didn't take place no one could get in or out of the great city. I'm not sure if all those invited to the meeting are still alive.

There were no flights back home, and all that remained to do was to listen to the reports and hope for a place on the first flight returning to Israel.

It was impossible to get away from the reports of the massacre in downtown Manhattan. The news was everywhere: on the air, at home, in the car, in the shops. I entered the neighborhood grocery store. The storekeeper's radio was on.

President Bush was speaking to the American people: "I declare tomorrow to be a day of prayer," said the President. "I ask every American, during lunch time tomorrow to pray for all the injured, their families, and the American nation. Go to church, to the synagogue, to the mosque and pray," ended the President.

"Did I hear right?" I ask the storekeeper, "Did he say mosque?"

She nodded.

"At this very moment you've just lost the war," I say to the astonished storekeeper, and start looking for what I need on the shelves. When the black boxes of the hijacked airplanes are recovered, we will hear the pilots screaming "Allahu Akbar" in the last moments before the crash. They slaughtered the Americans in the name of Allah, and now the President calls on them to pray to him.[1]

I wanted to shout what Moshe just said again and again : "At this very moment you've just lost the war – at this very moment you've just lost the war!"

God willing it's not too late for us, but Moshe sure has a point. The West and the Church have been defending themselves against a militant Islam for centuries and the Jews have been defending themselves against militant Palestinian Moslems ever since Israel became a nation. We in the West don't want to see this as a religious war, but it is, and this conflict won't go away. We may not hate Islam, but history irrefutably establishes that Islam has hated us ever since its inception. To Islam, we have always been the "infidels" and we will surely lose this war if we are unwilling to recognize who our enemies are and if we are reluctant to stand against them.

Arutz Sheva Israel National Radio, 9/24/2001, 4:51pm

Early this morning, Sal'it Sheetreet and her husband Barak, of Kibbutz Sdei Eliyahu, were attacked by Arab terrorist gunfire while traveling on the main northern Jordan Valley highway. Sal'it, 28 years of age, was killed almost instantly by gunfire to her head and was buried in the Sdei Eliyahu cemetery. Barak, the driver, was lightly injured by ricocheted fragments. Islamic Jihad claimed responsibility for the murder.

---

[1] All quotes in the preface are from www.arutz-7@israelnationalnews.com and they are quoted by permission.

Arutz Sheva Israel National Radio, 10/4/2001, 10:21am

In Jerusalem, an Arab car overtook that of a young Jewish couple, Pinchas and Mali Cohen of Ramat Shlomo, on one of the city's main highways, shot at the two, and sped off towards Ramallah. The attack occurred shortly before midnight on the road leading from Ramot and Ramat Shlomo towards French Hill. The young mother, pregnant with her second child, was shot in the chest and neck; she was originally reported as seriously wounded, but her condition is now listed as moderate, as is her husband, who was shot in the chest.

Ariel Sharon, Prime Minister of Israel
Excerpt of a Speech to the Knesset, September 4th 2001

"Today, Israel suffered another heinous Palestinian terrorist attack (in Afula), which took a heavy toll: Three dead and seven wounded. All our efforts to reach a cease-fire have been torpedoed by the Palestinians. The fire did not cease, not even for one day."

If you think those are just isolated incidents being quoted to inflame our passions, you would be wrong. This book could be filled with such accounts. Terrorist attacks are a daily occurrence in Israel, usually against civilian targets.

This is not just a view of the future, this is today and terrorism has come to us – the fall of the World Trade Center – the saber rattling of the anti-western Islamic states – the increased activism of Islamic radicals. These may well be the first shots of Armageddon – the beginning of the end – with final fulfillment of all Bible prophecy near at hand.

Arutz Sheva Israel National Radio, 9/30/2001, 8:19am
Palestinian Mufti Forbids Moslems to Join Anti-terror Coalition

The Middle East Media Research Institute reports that the Palestinian Authority Mufti in Jerusalem has called upon Moslems not to join the American anti-terrorism coalition. This past Friday, Sept. 28, 2001, the PA's Mufti, Sheikh

Ikrimah Sabri, encouraged the worshippers in the Al-Aqsa Mosque on the Temple Mount to oppose the coalition.

So much for any serious cooperation from Islamic mullahs. Even as we write, the mullahs in Pakistan and elsewhere are inflaming their local people against the United States' drive to destroy the terrorist cells in Afghanistan, but that behavior is nothing new. Major Bible prophecies, written 600 years before Muhammad was born, tell of the extreme enmity Islam will have towards Christendom. The Bible predicts Islam's militant rise to power during the Dark Ages and its decline after the battles of Tours and Vienna. The Bible also predicts the number of years that Moslems will control the Holy Land. The Bible then describes Islam's second rise to world influence after the return of the Jews to the Holy Land in 1948 – a Jihad we see before us now. The Bible finally predicts how this conflict will end.

What the Bible tells us about Islam and our final battle is the story, and it needs to be told. We may not be at war with Islam, but Islam has been at war with us for over 1300 years, in fact, ever since the First Jihad, which began in the 7th Century. The Bible tells us all about this war by predicting when the Moslem Dome of the Rock would be built in Jerusalem and when the Jewish people would be restored to the Holy Land. The events of 688, 1948 and 1967AD cannot be challenged.

The fulfillment of 1290 days of Dan 12:11 in the construction of the Dome of the Rock on the old temple mount is pinned to the beginning of the reign of Nebuchadnezzar, and few argue the 606BC or 605BC dating of that event.

That the restoration of the Jews to Israel in 1948 and the freeing of Jerusalem from Gentile domination in 1967 was predicted right to the year is unshakable.

That the time of Gentile dominion in Jerusalem is over is a plain declaration of Scripture, Luk 21:24. That we are in the "end-times" is easily concluded when that verse is compared with Dan 12:4, 9.

That the beasts, heads, and horns of Revelation 13 and 17 are empires and kingdoms, rather than an antichrist and his followers, has solid scriptural and historic foundation. That the final enemies of the church will come from the Islamic world is beyond reasonable doubt.

It cannot be biblically argued that the church will be taken to be with the Lord at any trumpet other than the very last trumpet of all time. Consequently, any position that requires trumpets to blow after the Last Trumpet of 1Co 15:51-52 is openly opposed to Scripture.

Wanting to keep this book simple, much of the supporting theological data has been left out. It there is sufficient interest, that data will be published in a second book. Reconciling all the data available for some of the concepts contained in this book has been a monumental task, so it would have been easy to overlook some relevant historic point or passage in Scripture. This could have lead to incorrect conclusions. We trusted the Holy Spirit to protect us from omission or excess.

The author takes the responsibility of writing a work on the Word of God very seriously. We fear God too much to willfully, or through carelessness, become just another heretic who led the church astray. Consequently, great care has been taken to be as historically accurate as possible, and to handle the Word of God with honor, humility and reverence, "rightly dividing the word of truth."

EHS

The Great Detective

CHAPTER 1

This people draw near me
with their mouth,
and with their lips do honour me,
but have removed their heart far from me,
and their fear toward me is taught
by the precept of men.

ISA 29:13

ALL of us have read a mystery. We find clues along the way and part of the fun in reading a mystery is in trying to solve it. None of us is ever smart enough to do so, of course, so in the final chapter a brilliant detective solves the crime, calls in the police, and the miserable felon is carted off to the slammer.

1 Cor 2:7 But we speak the wisdom of God in a mystery, *even* the hidden *wisdom,* which God ordained before the world.

Hummm ... the Greek word for mystery, *musterion,* appears 27 times in the New Testament, so part of the Bible is a mystery. Now much of God's mystery has been explained in the first 65 books of the Bible, but not all. The mere fact that there are so many confusing doctrines around is proof that we really haven't got it all figured out. So where can we find a detective that can solve the rest of God's mystery for us?

Rev 1:1 The **Revelation**[1] of Jesus Christ, which God gave unto him, to show unto his servants things which must shortly come to pass; and he sent and signified it by his angel unto his servant John.

For 2000 years, we have been trying to solve God's mystery on our own. We have poured over Scriptures, finding this clue and that, and with magnifying glass in hand have gone to Revelation to see if we could figure out that book as well, as if Revelation was part of the mystery. But from the above verse, it is apparent that Revelation isn't part of the mystery. It's Jesus' solution! God gave us a Great Detective in the person of His Son.

Rev 22:10 And he saith unto me, Seal not the sayings of the prophecy of this book: for the time is at hand.

Folks, have we been looking at Revelation through the wrong end of the telescope? Have we been going to Revelation with our doctrines in hand, trying to interpret that book through the filter of what we already believe? What if we stand behind Revelation and look back at the rest of Scripture through the grid of what Jesus might reveal to us in that book? If so, might Revelation emerge as Jesus' unraveling of the mystery of God's dealings with man throughout the ages? Might we be able to see the Jews, the church, the tribulation, and the Middle Eastern terrorists in a whole new light? Let's find out.

A Short History

At the end of the Middle Ages, the Church had fallen into a dead formalism that ushered in the Great Reformation. Many Roman Catholic Priests, some long forgotten, Eckhart, Tauler, Rokycana, Briconnet, Huss and the rest, were used of God to begin a great spiritual revival. At the time, every one of those early evangelists was considered a radical cultist by the established

---

[1] PUBLISHER'S NOTE: Occasionally the author has boldfaced a few words or a phrase in a Bible quote to draw your attention to a central subject. Such boldfacing does *not* appear in the original Bible texts.

church. Those excommunicate priests taught fanatically "heretical" doctrinal systems like salvation "by grace through faith," believer baptism and communion of both bread and cup for all believers. New converts followed those "left wing extremist" elder brethren, supporting their "heretical" positions, and almost before you knew it, those reformation groups became new denominations.

Five hundred years have passed, and those extremists have become us: the Baptists, the Presbyterians, the Lutherans, the Free Methodists – the whole Protestant evangelical world. The worthy elders of our denominations passed their views on down to us, and most of them are still taught today. And their views were generally sound, until ... until it came to Bible prophecy.

Among other unlikely concepts, the Leopard-Bear-Lion beast, the Beast with Two Horns, and the Scarlet Beast of Revelation were thought to be real live animals that would roam the earth. When those prophetic doctrines were in style, England was the great world power that spanned the globe and the sun never set on the British flag. Europe was the cultural center of the universe and the United States was but a minor nation full of woodsmen and farmers. In their wildest dreams, theologians of horse-and-buggy days couldn't have imagined two 110 story glass covered buildings standing on an island for which the Dutch paid $24, much less, that those buildings would be destroyed by ten Islamic terrorists using commercial airplanes as flying bombs.

If we are honest with ourselves, we can see that the end-time scenarios those venerable theologians proposed just don't fit what is happening in the world today. It is evident to all that we are at the end of the Christian Era, but as yet, there is no *visible* one-world government, no antichrist, and no Seven-Year Tribulation in sight. Is it possible that the Lord's plan for the end-times is totally different from the traditions we learned in Sunday school? It surely could be, because the Lord appears to have opened His prophetic Word in a new way through two almost unbelievable fulfillments of prophecy that have taken place in the Holy Land during the last 50 years:

In 1948AD, the new nation of Israel was established and in 1967, Jerusalem again came under Jewish control for the first time in 2573 years!

Though they were dispersed from their land for two millennia and persecuted beyond measure, the Jews again control the Holy Land and Jerusalem is again the capital of a sovereign nation called Israel. In the following chapters, we will show that these two events fulfill more prophecy than any other events since the crucifixion and these events allow us to understand Scriptures that were previously a mystery to us. Scriptures that change our view of God's overall plan and of how He intends to bring this age to a close. It is apparent that a rocky road lies ahead for Christians everywhere before Jesus stands on Zion. Spiritual storm clouds already loom on the horizon and there are questions that need to be answered ...

Will a worldwide holocaust against Jews and Christians soon take place and if so, can we escape it? How long will it last? Where would the Lord have us be while it is here and how will that time of trouble come to an end?

When Are We?

CHAPTER 2

When it is evening, ye say,
It will be fair weather: for the sky is red.
And in the morning, It will be foul weather to day:
for the sky is red and lowering.
O ye hypocrites, ye can discern the face of the sky;
but can ye not discern the signs of the times?

MAT 16:2-3

God sees creation from an eternal viewpoint and if we wish to understand His plan, we need to view it from His eternal perspective. If we could stand on a giant mountain somewhere and view our 6000+ years of recorded history all at once, as God does, we would see a broad completed tapestry. On that tapestry would be every event that has ever happened, or ever will happen. Time and space are creations of God and He stands outside them all:

> Isa 45:12 I have made the earth, and created man upon it: I, *even* my hands, have stretched out the heavens, and all their host have I commanded.

Man, however, is bound by time and space. We are physically placed on a material world and, as time is reckoned, the first decade of the 3rd Millennium AD. The Lord told us about all this in the Bible, and the Lord has partitioned his dealings with man into three separate time frames (three different spiritual epochs), each lasting about 2000 years. 1. The era before the flood, 2. the era between the flood and Jesus' crucifixion, 3. and the Christian Era. In each of these eras, God revealed Himself to man in a special way. In this chapter, we will be focusing our attention on the time that Gentiles controlled Jerusalem, the "Time of the Gentiles."

GRAPH NUMBER 1
Partial History of Israel
(from the time of Moses to the cross)

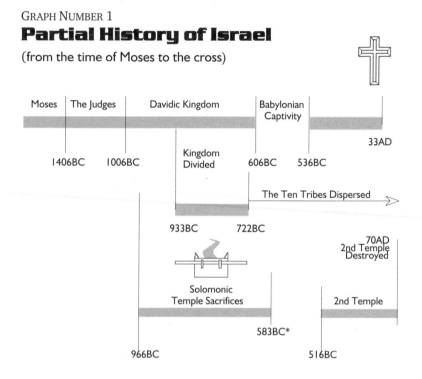

* Conservative dating places the destruction of the Temple of Solomon at 586BC. However, Jeremiah 41:5 shows Levitical sacrifices continuing to be offered long after that date:

> Jer 41:5 That there came certain from Shechem, from Shiloh, and from Samaria, *even* fourscore men, having their beards shaven, and their clothes rent, and having cut themselves, with offerings and incense in their hand, to bring *them* to the house of the LORD.

Jer 41:5 is positioned at the end of the governorship of Gedeliah, and Gedeliah was elevated to that post after Nebuchadnezzar sacked Jerusalem in 586BC. The sacrifices above were offered seven to ten months later. After Gedeliah's time, Jews were taken captive to Babylon only once more:

> Jer 52:30 In the three and twentieth year of Nebuchadnezzar, Nebuzaradan the captain of the guard carried away captive of the Jews seven hundred forty and five persons: all the persons *were* four thousand and six hundred.

Nebuchadnezzar's 1st year was 606-605BC, and this final captivity took place in the 23rd Year of Nebuchadnezzar, so we have scriptural support that 583BC was the date of the abolition of Levitical sacrifices. 606BC - 23 = 583BC.

This Christian Era actually began at the crucifixion, 32-33AD. Just before Jesus went to the cross, He told His disciples what they should expect this era to be like. Known to us as the "Olivet Discourse," this talk was Jesus' chapter-long prophecy about the major events that would take place between the Cross and His second coming. This discourse is recorded in the three synoptic Gospels: in Mat 24, Mar 13, and in Luk 21. Though these accounts all agree, each Gospel gave us some important information that is not contained in the other two:

(1) Mat 24:31 - Matthew states that the elect are gathered at the sound of a "great trumpet."

(2) Mar 13:14 - Mark declares that the Abomination of Desolation is an "it," and not a "him."

(3) Luk 21:24 - Luke defines the "time of the Gentiles."

Now please study those verses in your own Bible, and consider what Jesus had to say in each, because they strongly influence what we believe about the seven-year tribulation, replacement theology, and a host of other doctrines the church holds today. For instance, we hear a lot about the dispensations of "Law" and of "Grace," but in Luk 21:24, Jesus defines our era in a different way, as a "time of the Gentiles":

Luk 21:21-24 (*excerpts*) Then let them [*the Jews*] which are in Judaea flee ... And they [*the Jews*] shall fall by the edge of the sword, and **shall be** led away captive into all nations: and Jerusalem shall be trodden down of the Gentiles, until the **times of the Gentiles** be fulfilled.[1]

So what is this "time of the Gentiles"? When Jesus spoke those words (in 32 or 33AD), Jerusalem had already been under the

---

[1] PUBLISHER'S NOTE: Words or phrases [*in brackets and italics*] inserted within a Scripture quote are this author's explanation or amplification of a passage, usually discernable by context. Words [*in brackets and italics*] are not in the original Bible texts.

control of various Gentile governments for about 638 years.[1] But Jews troubled their foreign rulers with revolt after revolt, so in 70AD, Titus the Roman destroyed Jerusalem and burned the 2nd temple to the ground. Jesus foretold the destruction of the city and a time of Gentile domination of Jerusalem to follow. Look at the tense of the verb "shall be" led away captive. Shall be is future to when Jesus spoke.

After Titus destroyed Jerusalem, the Jews lost all control of their homeland and they were dispersed among the nations. They remained dispersed throughout the world until this very century. As a matter of historic record, Gentiles ruled Jerusalem through the 1st, 2nd, 3rd, 4th, 5th, 6th, 7th, 8th, 9th, and 10th centuries. The 11th and 12th century crusaders were also Gentiles. Gentiles continued to rule Jerusalem through the 13th, 14th, 15th, 16th, 17th, 18th, 19th, and 20th centuries, right on up until 1967AD. Throughout the whole Christian Era, Gentiles have always ruled Jerusalem. "And Jerusalem shall be trodden down of the Gentiles ... *until* ." As a matter of historic reality, the city of Jerusalem did not again come under Jewish control *until* after the Six-Day War, June 6th, 1967, "*until* the times of the Gentiles be fulfilled." The only people who are not Gentiles are Jews, and as of June 6th, 1967, the Jews again govern Jerusalem, for the first time in 2573 years. Like it or not, that is reality:[2]

---

[1] Rome was the foreign government in control of the Holy Land during Jesus' stay here on Earth, but Gentile control of Jerusalem began when Nebuchadnezzar of Babylon sacked the city in 606-605BC. Gentile rule continued under Medo-Persia and Greece. The Holy Land did not come under Roman jurisdiction until 65BC.

[2] The Jews had a short period of self-rule under the Maccabees that began in 167BC. However, the Maccabean period does not appear to be prophetically significant. The Davidic monarchy was not reestablished, and the Jews were continually in conflict with the Syrian Greeks. This conflict continued until Rome conquered the Holy Land in 65BC.

Over in the Holy Land is a nation called Israel. It is filled with a people called Jews, many of whom are looking for their Messiah. Those people again ruling in their own land fits the Luk 21:24 prophecy right to the letter.

Before the Six-Day War, we could argue about what the Lord might have meant by the "time of the Gentiles," but not anymore. From our vantage point in history, we can now see the Jews in control of Jerusalem with our own eyes. Consequently, it is apparent that the Lord was naming the total time of Gentile rule of His Holy City as "the Time of the Gentiles." Do we grasp the full impact of that prophecy? The time of the Gentile domination of Jerusalem is over. It's over! Gentiles will not rule in Jerusalem again, and God's eyes are again focused on the physical seed of Abraham who have returned to their promised land and now control the Holy City.

But if the "Time of the Gentiles" is really over, *when* are we now? What kind of time are we in? There must be another kind of time because we are still here. Searching Scripture from beginning to end, there appears to be only one other time that can come after the time of the Gentiles:

Dan 12:4 But thou, O Daniel, shut up the words, and seal the book, even to **the time of the end**.

Dan 12:9 And he said, Go thy way, Daniel: for the words are closed up and sealed till **the time of the end**.

Since we are no longer in the time of the Gentiles (and we have to be in some kind of time), then we are probably in Daniel's "time of the end," or the "end times" as the NASB translates it. As a result ...

We are probably the last generation this present Earth will ever see and the end of all things is at hand.

GRAPH NUMBER 2

Time of The Gentiles

Luk 21:24 And they [*the Jews*] shall fall by the edge of the sword, and shall be led away captive into all nations: and Jerusalem shall be trodden down of the Gentiles, until the times of the Gentiles be fulfilled.

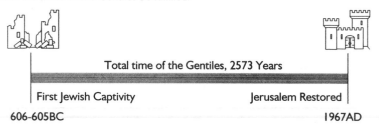

Total time of the Gentiles, 2573 Years

First Jewish Captivity   Jerusalem Restored

606-605BC   1967AD

DISCERNING END-TIME ERROR

In Dan 12:9, God declared, by His sovereign Word, that He sealed the book of Daniel until the time of the end. Sealed it, which means that nobody would be able to understand it. That doesn't sound so earth-shattering, does it? How significant can it be that a relatively obscure Old Testament prophet would be sealed until the time of the end? This important:

> *If the "Time of the End" began in 1967, and Daniel was sealed until the "Time of the End," then all views theorized out of Daniel before 1967 would at best be incomplete, and at worst be heretical.*

Here is the point: Most end-time views held by the Church today were theorized from studies made in Daniel hundreds of years ago. But if God sealed Daniel until the "time of the end," and the "time of the end" didn't begin until 1967, then those end-time views have to be incomplete, or even wrong. If they are, we could be basing the last few decisions we will ever make on this planet on theoretical events that are never going to take place. So let's take a look at the book of Daniel, from which so many of our popular end-time doctrines have come.

69 Weeks

CHAPTER 3

Remember the former things of old;
for I am God, and there is none else;
I am God, and there is none like me,
Declaring the end from the beginning,
and from ancient times
the things that are not yet done.

ISA 46:9-10

DURING the last two thousand years, many schools of prophetic thought have been proposed, but the Jews returning to the Holy Land in 1948, and Jerusalem being freed of Gentile domination in 1967, open the door to a new understanding of the prophetic Scriptures that was hidden from the Church throughout the Christian Era. Since Daniel wasn't opened until the end-times, every one of those earlier views are at best, questionable. The popular view, that a great tribulation will come at the end of this age began with an 18th Century Jesuit priest's studies in Daniel. He based his conclusions on the prophecies in Daniel 9 and 12 that contain time frames of weeks and days.

But the question is this: Are the prophetic "days" in Daniel and Revelation actually 24-hour days, as some suppose, or do they represent some totally different duration of time? There are sound reasons to believe those "days" and "weeks" actually symbolize Hebrew years. We can find out for sure from the 70 Weeks of Daniel 9, where both the starting point of a prophecy, and its fulfillment, are events that have already happened . Events that we can read about in history.

DANIEL RECEIVES A MESSENGER

Darius the Mede conquered Babylon in 536BC. By that time, Daniel and his people had been captive in Babylon for 70 years. Daniel knew from a prophecy in the book of Jeremiah that their time of captivity should be over:

> Jer 29:10 For thus saith the LORD, "That after seventy years be accomplished at Babylon I will visit you, and perform my good word toward you, in causing you to return to this place."

The night Babylon fell must have been some kind of night. Earlier that evening, Daniel had interpreted the handwriting on the wall and King Belshazzar promoted him to the post of third ruler of the empire.[1] What did it matter that Darius' army was right outside the walls? The walls of Babylon were impregnable and there was plenty of food in store. The Babylonians couldn't run out of water because the whole Euphrates River ran right through the city, under the city walls. They were so confident in their defenses that they never even imagined the possibility of an invasion. The Babylonians were feasting and drinking and having a fabulous revel, or so they thought (Dan 5:1-4).

But upriver from the city, Darius dug a canal that diverted the whole Euphrates River and he marched his army into the city on the dry riverbed. It was an easy victory and King Belshazzar was slain (Dan 5:30).

In this new Medo-Persian Empire, Daniel was again just an ordinary citizen. So what would happen to his people under this new regime? They had now been captives in Babylon for 70 years.

---

[1] Belshazzar, son of Nabonidus, reigned as co-regent of the Babylonian Empire under his father (552-536BC). During the Medo-Persian invasion, Nabonidus was traveling in Arabia and Belshazzar was ruling the city during his absence. So "third ruler of the land" was the highest post to which Daniel could be elevated as long as both Belshazzar and Nabonidus were alive.

Daniel's night in the lions' den and his promotion to the post of chief satrap were still some time in the future.

Daniel went home to read Scripture and pray. That prayer of Daniel's wasn't some little routine kind of prayer like: "Oh Lord, thank you for our food, in Your Name we pray, Amen." He fasted and sat in sackcloth and ashes, probably for days (Dan 9:3). He must have thought for a long time about what he was going to say, and then written down his prayer, for surely, this is one of the most eloquent prayers in all Scripture. Here is part of what Daniel prayed:

> Dan 9:16-19 O Lord, according to all thy righteousness, I beseech thee, let thine anger and thy fury be turned away from thy city Jerusalem, thy holy mountain. Because for our sins, and for the iniquities of our fathers, Jerusalem and thy people are become a reproach to all that are about us. Now therefore, O our God, hear the prayer of thy servant, and his supplications, and cause thy face to shine upon thy sanctuary that is desolate, for the Lord's sake. O my God, incline thine ear, and hear; open thine eyes, and behold our desolations, and the city which is called by thy name: for we do not present our supplications before thee for our righteousnesses, but for thy great mercies. O Lord, hear; O Lord, forgive; O Lord, hearken and do; defer not, for thine own sake, O my God: for thy city and thy people are called by thy name.

Daniel confessed his sins and the sins of his people. This elderly man of God knew that he and the rest of the Jews deserved nothing from God, any more than we do. But considering the Lord's great mercy, and because of His word through Jeremiah, weren't the 70 years of captivity over?

While Daniel was praying, God sent the angel Gabriel to comfort him, and because the 70 years of captivity were indeed over, to tell him of a new and different 70: a future seventy of sevens. Here is what Gabriel told him:

> Dan 9:24-26 Seventy weeks [or *sevens*] are determined upon thy people and upon thy holy city, to finish the transgression,

and to make an end of sins, and to make reconciliation for iniquity, and to bring in everlasting righteousness, and to seal up the vision and prophecy, and to anoint the most Holy. Know therefore and understand, *that* from the going forth of the commandment to restore and to build Jerusalem unto the Messiah the Prince *shall be* seven weeks [*or sevens*], and threescore and two weeks [*or sevens*]: the street shall be built again, and the wall, even in troublous times. And after threescore and two weeks [*or sevens*] shall Messiah be cut off, but not for himself.

The Bible is a historic book. Each book within it was written at a specific time and records events that took place in history. In the same way, Bible prophecy was written at a given time in history, to be fulfilled at a specific time in the future. Those points in time are usually stated in Scripture, as they were in the 70 Weeks. "From the going forth of the commandment" is the definite starting time for that prophecy, and "and after the three score and two weeks" is the definite fulfillment time. If we wish to understand how long those weeks are, we need to see if the events prophesied have taken place, and measure the time that passed between the issuing of the prophecy and its fulfillment.

The 70 Weeks is divided into three sections: Seven Weeks, Sixty-two Weeks and One Week. Let's look at the 69 weeks first. To whom are they addressed and what are they about? They are to the Jews, and about Jerusalem. What does v. 24 tell us will be accomplished in those 69 sevens?

1. "Finish transgression."
2. "Make an end of sin."
3. "Make reconciliation for iniquity."
4. "Bring in everlasting righteousness."
5. "Seal up vision and prophecy."
6. "To anoint the most Holy."

When will they take place, and what is the time frame? We are told to start counting time after a decree is sent out to restore Jerusalem, and that it will be a time of trouble.

There were four restoration decrees granted by the Medo-Persian Empire. But almost 100 years after Gabriel spoke to Daniel, a special decree was granted by Artaxerxes I to Nehemiah (444-445BC). This is the ONLY decree recorded in the Bible that gave the Jews permission to "restore Jerusalem and rebuild its walls," and since Scripture relates to Scripture, we should start counting time from that biblical decree. Just as Daniel predicted, Nehemiah had a terrible time wall-building.[1] The people living around Jerusalem tried to stop him every way they could (Neh 4:1-23). They even tried to get the government to come down on him, just as the unsaved and pseudo-Christians try to come down on true Christians today. The Messiah is Jesus, of course, and He was crucified in 32 or 33AD. He didn't die for Himself, but for the sins of the whole world (1Jo 2:2), but are those 69 weeks 69 sevens of years? If so, then we have 69 x 7 or 483 Hebrew years.

The Lord usually spoke to His prophets in a language they could understand. Daniel was a Jew, probably of the royal family (2Ki 20:18), and the Jews had their own 360-day Levitical year. Since our history is recorded in solar years of 365.24 days, we need to convert 483 Hebrew years to solar years:

$$483 \times .9857 = 476 \text{ solar years.} \text{ [2]}$$

---

[1] The whole book of Nehemiah is about events following the Artaxerxes I decree. Furthermore, the events recorded in Nehemiah perfectly match Daniel's prophecy of them. The dating of this decree is firm at 445-444BC.

[2] From I Maccabees and the Book of Jubilees (circa 150BC), the Jews of inter-testamental times generally considered a month to have 30 days, and a year to have12 months. So a year of 360 days was probably the calendar with which Daniel was familiar. That is why a year of 360 days should be used when calculating O.T. prophecies.

    The moon circuits the earth in about 29.12 days, forcing a vacillation between a 30-day and a 29-day month. Twelve of these lunar months equal 354.14 days, or about eleven days short of the solar year. From the Babylonians

GRAPH NUMBER 3

The 69 Weeks

Dan 9:24 (KJV) Seventy weeks are determined upon thy people and upon thy holy city, to finish the transgression, and to make an end of sins, and to make reconciliation for iniquity, and to bring in everlasting righteousness, and to seal up the vision and prophecy, and to anoint the most Holy. Know therefore and understand, *that* from the going forth of the commandment to restore and to build Jerusalem unto the Messiah the Prince *shall be* seven weeks, and threescore and two weeks: the street shall be built again, and the wall, even in troublous times. And after threescore and two weeks shall Messiah be cut off, but not for himself: and the people of the prince that shall come shall destroy the city and the sanctuary; and the end thereof *shall be* with a flood, and unto the end of the war desolations are determined.

From the Decree of Artaxerxes I, to the cross

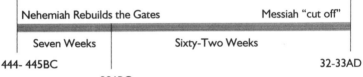

Nehemiah Rebuilds the Gates	Messiah "cut off"
Seven Weeks	Sixty-Two Weeks
444- 445BC	32-33AD

396BC
Old Testament Canon closes

7 Weeks =48.3 yrs, 62 Weeks = 427.7 yrs. Total time 476 yrs.

Note: Historical dates are recorded in Solar years, so for O.T. prophecy it is necessary to convert from the Hebrew year of 360 days to a solar year of 365.24 days. The conversion factor is .9857. (See Graph on p. 37). To keep the math simple, the absence of the zero year is ignored. Late evidence indicates that the Artaxerxes I decree could have been issued as early as 445BC, while other evidence indicates that the Lord was crucified not earlier than 32AD and possibly as late as 34AD. This one to three year ambiguity gives wide latitude for scholarly differences on the exact dating of these events, but does not negate the historic fit of this prophecy. Regardless of man's faulty record of these historic events, it was still 483 Hebrew years from the Artaxerxes I decree to the cross.

---

the Hebrews learned to add an extra month every two or three years. In rabbinical times this "intercalary" month was inserted seven times in nineteen years. From *Calendar*, (Holman's Bible Dictionary).

Artaxerxes' decree, 444BC + 476 years = 32AD, the cross right to the year!

The cross, right to the year. But what about those six points that were supposed to be fulfilled during these 70 weeks? Aa-ha! All but one were fulfilled at the cross. Did not Jesus (1) finish transgression eternally, (2) make an end of sin, (3) make reconciliation for iniquity, (4) bring in everlasting righteousness, and (6) anoint the Most holy with His own precious blood.[1] Of course, praise the Lord! Point (5), however, was left out: "Seal up vision and prophecy." This is where those peculiar 7 weeks and 62 weeks come in:

7 x 7 Hebrew years = 48.3 Solar years. 444BC - 48.3 is 395.7BC, Malachi written.

Malachi was inspired to write the last book of the Old Testament in about 396BC. The Scripture to the Jews was complete, and no more was written until the New Testament era! So Old Testament vision and prophecy were indeed "sealed up." As one dear Rabbi lamented in about 200BC, "The Holy Spirit has departed from Israel," and until this very day, the Jews, as a nation, have not been permitted to see any further. The Lord has blinded their eyes so they could not recognize Jesus as their Messiah (Rom 11:8, 2Co 3:15).

---

[1] Incredible as it may sound, it appears that the archeologist Ron Wyatt may have found the Ark of the Covenant. According to Wyatt, the Ark was hidden in a cave under Golgotha – Gordon's Calvary. From the Word of the Lord to him, Jeremiah knew that Jerusalem was about to fall, so he appears to have placed the Table of Showbread, the Altar of Incense, and the Ark of the Covenant in that cave and walled them up. The cave was forgotten, and these articles have remained secreted ever since. This explains a previously inexplicable prophecy: "and He shall anoint the Most Holy." During the crucifixion, Jesus' side was pierced, and the rocks beneath the cross rent (Mat 27:51). According to Wyatt, the Ark is about 20 feet under where the Lord was crucified. It appears that Jesus' blood ran through a fissure in the bedrock and fell on the Mercy Seat. If so, then in accordance with Dan 9:24, Jesus did indeed "anoint the Most Holy" with His own precious blood. Videotapes and various newsletters are available from Wyatt Archeological Research, 713 Lambert Dr. Nashville, TN 37220. World Net Daily, www.wnd.com also has information on Wyatt in its archives. Search Ron Wyatt.

THE DAY=YEARS

So what have we learned so far? Not only that 69 Weeks were fulfilled at the cross, but also that those "weeks" were not ordinary weeks of days at all, but weeks of years. Every single day of those 69 weeks represented a Hebrew year, and we can prove it through known historical events. There are even three verses in Scripture that back up the day=year interpretation.

Captive with Daniel in the province of Babylon was a priest named Ezekiel. He was the prophet inspired by the Lord to write the canonical book that bears his name. We can see that Daniel read Scripture in his devotions (Dan 9:2). He studied Jeremiah, so no doubt he also studied the other Scriptures that were available to him, including the books of Numbers and Ezekiel. Within those two books are three verses that gave him the insight he needed to understand prophetic day=years:

> Num 14:34 After the number of the days in which ye searched the land, even forty days, **each day for a year**.

> Eze 4:5-6 For I have laid upon thee the years... according to the number of the days, three hundred and ninety days ... so shalt thou bear the iniquity of the house of Israel ... and thou shalt bear the iniquity of the house of Judah forty days: I have appointed thee **each day for a year**.

A day for a year. Here, in the only two places it appears in the Bible, the Lord showed Daniel that one prophetic day was equal to one of our earthly years. ONE DAY = ONE YEAR! Using this day=year unit of measure to interpret his prophecies, Daniel could not only understand the 69 weeks of Dan 9, but also the 1290 and 1335 days of Dan 12. If we use the same unit of measure that Daniel did, we should be able to understand those day=years as well.

This is not a new concept in the Church. In 1569, the great Anabaptist theologian, Thieleman van Braght, wrote the following in *Martyrs Mirror,* pages 21-24:

GRAPH NUMBER 4

The Day = Year Principle

Ezek 4:5 (KJV) For I have laid upon thee the years of their iniquity, according to the number of the days, three hundred and ninety days: so shalt thou bear the iniquity of the house of Israel.

Ezek 4:6 (KJV) And when thou hast accomplished them, lie again on thy right side, and thou shalt bear the iniquity of the house of Judah forty days: I have appointed thee each day for a year.

One Day | One Year

(In the O.T., Hebrew 360 day. In the N.T., Solar 365.24 day)

After the day=year revelation was given to Ezekiel, when "days" are spoken of in a prophetic sense, they should be viewed either as Hebrew or Solar years unless context clearly dictated otherwise. The day=year interpretation is scriptural, and it is not hermeneutically sound to view prophetic days differently unless an intervening Scripture annulled that principle.

Hebrew Year = 360 days, or .9857 Solar year: ONLY for interpreting Old Testament prophecy. Daniel used the Hebrew calendar.

The moon circuits the earth in about 29.12 days, forcing a vacillation between a 30-day and a 29-day month. Twelve of these lunar months equal 354.14 days, or about eleven days short of the solar year. From the Babylonians the Hebrews learned to add an extra month every two or three years. In rabbinical times this "intercalary" month was inserted seven times in nineteen years. From *Calendar*, (Holman's Bible Dictionary).

From I Maccabees and the Book of the Jubilees it appears that Jews of intertestimental times generally considered a month to be 30 days, and a year to be 360 days. Consequently, this was probably the calendar with which Daniel was familiar so it is the one we use to interpret O.T. day=years.

Solar Year = 365.24 days: ONLY for interpreting New Testament prophecy. John was under Roman rule and used the solar calendar.

In the interest of simplicity, the zero year or lack thereof is ignored. Computations fall within the one to three year ambiguity in dates prior to the 1st Century.

"a thousand two hundred and threescore days, which, reckoned according to prophetic language **means as many years** ... let it be reckoned as it may, say we, as a very long period of time."

Two hundred years later, Matthew Henry, in his *Commentary on the Whole Bible,* came to the same conclusion (Vol VI, page 1157, column 1, para. 2):

" ... if the beginning of that interval could be ascertained, this number of prophetic days, taking **a day for a year**, would give us a prospect of when the end might be."

So we can now understand the day=year, but the concept is so important that it should be more fully explained. Daniel was raised under the Levitical code and the Jews had a twelve-month calendar, each of thirty days, for 360 day year. Consequently, it is correct to use a 360-day year to interpret Old Testament prophecies like his.[1] But since our records of ancient history are all in Solar Years of 365.24 days, we do need to convert those Hebrew 360 day=years to fit our records.[2]

The Apostle John, however, lived his whole life during the Christian Era, under a Gentile Roman government, and his book is primarily to the Gentile church. Consequently, it is proper to use the Gentile solar calendar of 365.24 days to interpret John's prophecies.

---

[1] Footnote on pp 33-34 gives further details on the Jewish calender.

[2] There is a generally accepted one to three year ambiguity in Babylonian empire dates. The interpretations of Daniel's prophecies proposed in this book fit within that window and are in fact the *conservative* dates for those events. Conservative church scholars date the 70 year Babylonian captivity from the beginning of the Jewish exile (606-605BC) to their return to the Holy Land (536BC), while orthodox rabbinical scholars date the Babylonian captivity from the destruction of the temple (586BC) to the building of the 2nd Temple (516BC). Both were periods of 70 years. However, the starting times of Daniel's day=year and "time, times" prophecies are tied to neither view of the captivity, but to the accession years of Nebuchadnezzar and Belshazzar as kings of Babylon (606BC and 552BC), and to the 3rd year that Cyrus reigned over that city (533BC).

1290 Days

CHAPTER 4

Be not ye like your fathers,
which trespassed against the
LORD God of their fathers,
who therefore gave them up
to desolation, as ye see.

2CH 30:7

WHEN I began this study of Revelation twenty-two years ago, what I really had in mind was finding scriptural support for the *Seven-Year Tribulation* view that I was so confidently teaching. I was just as convinced as everyone else that there was going to be one. So the surprise of my life came when I couldn't prove that view from Scripture. Major pillars of that view are the prophetic "days" of Dan 12:11-12. We now realize we should probably interpret those days as years. But if they are years, how do we know when they began or when they end? For that, we need look at *when* the Lord gave this prophecy to Daniel:

> Dan 10:1 In the third year of Cyrus the Persian, a thing was revealed unto Daniel ... but the appointed time was long: and he understood the thing, and had understanding of the vision.

Dan 10:1 to Dan 12:13 is the final vision of Daniel's prophetic ministry. The year was 533BC and the prophecy is obviously about the future of Daniel's people, the Jews then in captivity. A major portion of this prophecy is a detailed account of the Medo-Persian and Greek control of the Jews in the Holy Land during

Photo courtesy of Biblical Archeology Review

The Temple Mount as seen from the North. The Moslem memorial, the Dome of the Rock, stands in its center as it has for 1300 years. In the upper left is the Al Aqsa Mosque, considered by Moslems to be their 3rd most holy. Circled in the lower right is a little, unimposing cupola, the Dome of the Tablets. Late archeological evidence indicates that the Holy of Holies in both the Solomonic and the 2nd Temple was located here, some 330 feet north of the Dome itself. The Dome appears to be in what was once called the Court of the Gentiles.

the next 400 years. The Babylonian empire had fallen some three years earlier and Daniel was now a very old man, probably in his nineties. He had been a captive in Babylon for 73 years. According to Ezr 3:2, the Jews had just begun their trek back to the Holy Land under the leadership of a Jewish prince named Zerubbabel and a high priest named Jeshua. That is the historic setting for Daniel's final prophecy, within which is a curious passage about "times" and another about days:

> Dan 12:11 (NASB) And from the time that the regular sacrifice is abolished, and the abomination of desolation is set up, *there will be* **1,290 days**.

Curious, indeed. Are these prophetic "days" just ordinary twenty-four hour days, or could they be years again, like they were in the 69 weeks ... and if they are years, what is an "Abomination that maketh Desolate," as the King James calls it? Well, the verse refers to the "daily sacrifice" and since those sacrifices were only offered at the temple in Jerusalem, then temple sacrifices were probably involved. As a result, that abomination would have to be something done to God's temple site that would defile it and make it impossible for the priests to offer sacrifices there. It was true in Daniel's time and it is true now. God has not changed where sacrifices should be offered anywhere in the Bible.[1]

But to which abolition of sacrifices is the Lord referring in this "1290-day" prophecy? Now please, let's not try to make a New Testament doctrine out of this Old Testament Scripture. The

---

[1] The OT continually corrects Israel's people for offering on the "high places," instructing them to bring their offerings to the temple instead (2 Ch 28:24-25). Priests were authorized to sacrifice only on the Altar of Burnt Offering (Deu 12:10-14); so to the Jews, an Abomination that made Desolate would be anything that kept them from offering sacrifices on the temple site. Levitical law dictated that anyone who desecrated the temple was to be stoned with stones until dead. In defiance of this, a Greek king, Antiochus Epiphanies, sacrificed a pig on the altar of burnt offering (circa 168BC). That started the Maccabean revolt, and the incident has been known ever since as an "abomination that made desolate." After that desecration, the priests had to perform extensive purification of the altar before they could again offer sacrifices upon it.

addressees are clearly defined. It is in Hebrew, to the Jews. It is about the Holy Land while Gentile powers were ruling there. Context refers to "thy people" (Dan 12:1). Daniel was a Jew and the prophecy was given to him, so it is to and about the Jews during the Time of the Gentiles. There is no reason to believe the Lord was telling Daniel about an abolition of sacrifices that might take place 2500 years later, at the end of the Christian Era.

Sacrifices were suspended three times in the Old Testament: once before Daniel (2Ch 28:24-25), once during the Babylonian captivity (2Ch 36:19 and Ezr 3:6), and once, about four hundred years later, by the Greek king Antiochus Epiphanies. So to which event do you suppose the Lord might be referring?

Well, to whom was this prophecy given? To Daniel in 533BC. Result: we have every reason to believe that the Lord was referring to sacrifices that were abolished during Daniel's own lifetime: to an abolition of sacrifices *to which Daniel could relate!*

Was it at the time of destruction of the temple? It doesn't seem so. Nebuchadnezzar destroyed the temple in 586BC, but the prophet Jeremiah tells us that temple sacrifices continued long after the temple was burned:

> Jer 41:5 ... from Shechem, from Shiloh, and from Samaria, even fourscore men ... with offerings and incense in their hand, to bring them to the house of the LORD.

Those men came to the temple at the end of the governorship of Gedaliah (seven to ten months *after* the temple was burned), so there had to be some purified priests in Jerusalem who were still carrying on. Two more years pass, then in the very last chapter of Jeremiah we read:

> Jer 52:30 In the three and twentieth year of Nebuchadnezzar, Nebuzaradan the captain of the guard carried away captive of the Jews seven hundred forty and five persons.

Nebuchadnezzar ascended the throne of Babylon in 606-605BC. Twenty-three years later is 583BC. Therefore, this final captivity of 583BC is a scripturally supportable time for the sacrifices to have been abolished. Babylonians took the nobles, artisans and priests captive; they left only the poorest people in the land. There were apparently no purified priests left in the land who could offer sacrifices. What a devastating experience this must have been for God's people in captivity.

Oh, how the Jews repented. From the Babylonian captivity to this very day, they have not departed from the Lord their God, nor has an idol been seen among them. As a conquered people in exile, they had 70 years to regret their waywardness, and they never forgot it. Their repentance is poignantly recorded in this short quote from an unknown psalmist:

> *By the rivers of Babylon, there we sat down.*
> *Yea, we wept, when we remembered Zion.*
> *We hanged our harps*
> *upon the willows in the midst thereof.*
> *For there they that carried us away captive*
> *required of us a song;*
> *and they that wasted us required of us mirth, saying,*
> *Sing us one of the songs of Zion.*
> *How shall we sing the LORD's song*
> *in a strange land?*

PSA 137:1-4

Though he was hundreds of miles from Jerusalem, Daniel knew all about these new hostages. Another group of Jewish captives being brought back to Babylon by Nebuzaradan, captain of the king's guard, could not have escaped Daniel's notice.[1] He was daily in King Nebuchadnezzar's court (Dan 2:48-49). Oh, how it must have hurt that saintly man to hear of the sacrifices being stopped and of

---

[1] For details on the Babylonian captivity, please refer to Graph No.1 on p24. It cannot be positively proven from Jer 41.5 and 52:30 that sacrifices were abolished in 583BC. However, there are N.T. prophecies that give ample support for that date. These prophecies will be discussed in later chapters.

the Lord's temple in utter ruin. We can prove that the temple site was abandoned during Daniel's lifetime from Dan 9:17 and Ezr 3:2-3. With that historic background in place, let's look at Dan 12:11 again:

> Dan 12:11 And from the time that the regular sacrifice is abolished, and the abomination of desolation is set up, *there will be* **1,290 days**.

By applying the day=year unit of measure to that verse, Daniel could understand the vision. He remembered when the regular evening and morning sacrifices were abolished. He looked from that time on down 1290 Hebrew years into the future. He knew that an unbelievable abomination was going to trespass on the temple mount.[1] An atrocity that would make it desolate. The abomination to come would defile the site and prevent all future sacrifices. What could that terrible thing be? Daniel could not know, but we can because 1290 years since the sacrifices were abolished have already passed. They were over in 688AD.[2]

So what happened in 688AD? Well, from 685 to 705AD, the Moslem Kalifah, Abd el Malik ibn Marwan, built a memorial to Muhammad, the Dome of the Rock, on God's temple mount! Thus, we now have a positive identification:

The Dome of the Rock is the Abomination of Desolation!

---

[1] This is how Daniel could understand the vision. God gave the 1290-day vision fifty years *after* the regular sacrifices had been abolished. Looking back, Daniel could see that nothing of any special significance had taken place just 1290 ordinary days after their abolition, so he knew the Lord was speaking of something other than ordinary 24 hour days. Daniel then put together when sacrifices were abolished with the definition for prophetic days given by the prophet Ezekiel (Eze 4:6 "I have appointed thee each day for a year.") and saw that the abomination was still 1290 years in his future.

[2] Some may argue that sacrifices could have been abolished a year or two earlier, or a couple of years later than 583BC, as suggested by the author. But none argue that they were abolished earlier than the destruction of the temple (586BC), nor more than ten years later. The Dome of the Rock and Al-Aqsa Mosque were under construction on the temple mount for about 20 years, from 685 to 705AD. Leaving the widest latitude for scholarly argument, that 20-year window cannot be circumvented.

That is not just coincidence or suppositional theology. The day=year interpretation fits the words of Daniel 12:11 exactly and it fits known history TO THE YEAR. The construction date of the Dome of the Rock is a plain historic fact that you can prove for yourself from any good encyclopedia or world history.

And so, for the first time in Scripture, we run into the Moslems. Islam, and nobody else, was responsible for the construction of the Abomination that maketh Desolate![1]

That temple mount of God Most Holy was made spiritually desolate over 1300 years ago and it remains so today. The Jews can't offer sacrifices to the Lord on His holy mountain while that structure to THE false prophet remains there. That is why there is such an interest among conservative Jews about tearing it down. It is no secret to the Jewish Rabbis that the Dome of the Rock is an abomination that makes desolate. In the following chapters we will see how the New Testament fully supports the identity of the dome as the Abomination that maketh Desolate.

Now don't forget 688AD and the Dome of the Rock. We're going to run into that date, and Islam, again and again. And remember 583BC, too. Both dates are important.

---

[1] Jerry Landay in his book, *The Dome of the Rock* (Newsweek, New York, NY, 1972) p. 18, records that when Khalifah Omar entered Jerusalem in 639AD, he was met by Sophronius, Bishop of the Jerusalem Church, who showed him around the city. Seeing the temple mount (then in rubble), Omar declared that he was going to build a memorial to Muhammad on the original site of the temple of God. Sophronius exclaimed in horror, "Verily, this is the Abomination of Desolation as spoken of by Daniel the prophet, and it now stands in the holy place." Though Sophronius was a very old man of about 80, Khalifah Omar put him in prison and to forced labor, the severities of which killed him.

The Dome of the Rock being the Abomination that maketh Desolate is not a new theology. It's a truth that's been with the Church for over 1300 years, but somehow we have managed to forget the prophetic words of Sophronius, Bishop of the Jerusalem Church.

GRAPH NUMBER 5

Abomination of Desolation

Dan 12:11 (KJV) And from the time *that* the daily *sacrifice* shall be taken away, and the abomination that maketh desolate set up, *there shall be* a thousand two hundred and ninety days.

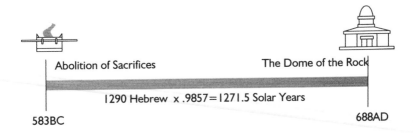

Abolition of Sacrifices   The Dome of the Rock

1290 Hebrew x .9857 = 1271.5 Solar Years

583BC   688AD

Note: Biblical day=year prophecies have a beginning date in history specified by context, and now we can see their historic fulfillments. In Mar 13:14 the Abomination of Desolation is referred to as an "it" not a him, and this dome, a Moslem structure, has now stood on God's temple mount for over 1300 years. There are now over a 1.2 billion people in that false religion, so Muhammad could certainly qualify as the false prophet of Rev 19:20. Best estimates are that 10-15 percent of Moslems worldwide are of the militant Islamic strain. That means over 100 million human beings are, to a greater or lesser degree, caught up in the world's most dangerous fanaticism. Since there are no less than three to five million Moslems in the US, we can reasonably conclude that somewhere between 300,000 to 750,000 American Moslems support the terrorists.

The Wrong Rock

CHAPTER 5

Behold ye among the heathen,
and regard, and wonder marvelously:
for I will work a work in your days,
which ye will not believe,
though it be told you.

HAB 1:5

FROM our position in the opening days of the 21st century, we can just begin to see a little of God's exquisite plan. The Abomination that maketh Desolate is not an antichrist in our future. It is an Islamic building that has stood on Mount Moriah for over 1300 years. But like the Lord said to Habakkuk, we wouldn't have believed Him if He had told us in advance, and now that we can see it, we can still hardly believe it.

LOCATING SOLOMON'S TEMPLE

The 1290 days of Daniel, when interpreted as years, fitting one incident in history is not sufficient evidence to prove that all prophetic "days" should be understood as years – even when the 1290 days hit an event as remarkable as the construction of the Dome of the Rock on Mount Moriah, *right to the year*. However, in Daniel's 70 Weeks, we saw that 69 of those weeks were really 69 weeks of years that were fulfilled at the cross. Since that is the prophetic time system the Lord used in one part of Scripture, wouldn't we need scriptural authorization to change it if we ran into prophetic days somewhere else? Wouldn't it be poor theology to leave a divinely ordained system that we can show works and try to interpret "days" in some other way, particularly since that would go against God's declaration, "I give you a day for a year"?

Location of the Solomonic Temple

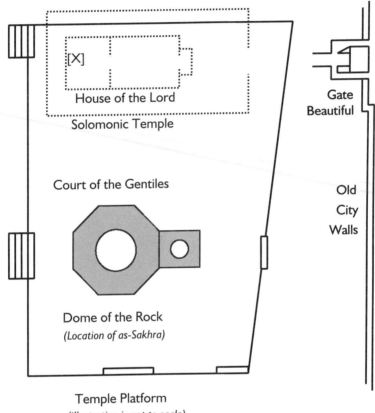

Temple Platform
(illustration is not to scale)

[X] Location of the flat bedrock, now under the Dome of the Tablets.

This sketch of the Temple Mount shows the Moslem *Dome of the Rock* to be some 330 feet south of the sites for both the Solomonic and 2nd temples. The dotted line shows the location of the Temple of Solomon. Notice that it faces East and is directly in line with the Golden Gate. The 2nd temple (not shown) was in the same location, but it faced 6° more easterly. In both temples, the flat bedrock, now under the little Dome of the Tablets, was part of the floor of the *Kodesh ha-Kodashim*, or Holy of Holies. Documentation for this drawing may be found in Biblical Archeology Review, March 1983.

Of course. So to stay in line with Scripture, we should at least look at the possibility of historic day=year fits for other prophetic "days" in Scripture.

Let's begin by imagining ourselves on the Isle of Patmos at the end of the 1st century, looking at the world about us through the eyes of the Apostle John as he writes Revelation. It is now about 70 years after Calvary and the Jews were in a state of revolt against their Roman rulers. That wasn't anything new. They had been in rebellion against Rome ever since their occupation began (65BC). Army after Roman army had been sent to the Holy Land to quell the continual uprisings, but they just kept happening. Losing all patience, Rome finally sent her best general against Jerusalem itself and the city was almost totally destroyed. An estimated 1,000,000 Jews fell to sword and famine and the beautiful Second Temple was torn down to bedrock. It had taken 45 years to build, but stone by stone the Romans threw it into the valleys of Tyropoeon and Kidron just as Jesus had prophesied 37 years earlier: "not one stone will be left standing upon another." His prophecy of the coming devastation is recorded in three places, Mat 24:2, Mar 13:2, and Luk 21:6.

The Christians in the city were aware of Jesus' prophecy, so just prior to that city's destruction they fled Jerusalem in haste. Early church records assert that no Christians were left in the city, and that no Christian lives were lost during the ensuing massacre.[1] The demolition of the temple was so complete that even the memory of its exact location was lost. Then, except for a short-

---

[1] Titus destroyed Jerusalem in 70AD. According to Tacitus, the city was crowded with 600,000 visitors. After five months the walls were battered down, the Temple burned, and the city was put to the sword. Josephus states that over 1,000,000 Jews were killed and 95,000 taken captive. Henry Halley, *Halley's Bible Handbook* (Grand Rapids, MI, Zondervan, 1965) pp. 655-656. However, Eusebius writes, "On the other hand, the people of the church in Jerusalem, were commanded by oracle given by revelation to those in the city who were worthy of it, to depart and dwell in one of the cities of Perea, which they called Pella." *Ecclesiastical History*, Book 3, v. 5, ln. 3-4.

lived temple of Jupiter, God's temple site remained in rubble for over 600 years.

However, in 685, the Moslem governor of Jerusalem, one Kalifah Abd el Malik ibd Marwan, began clearing the temple mount. He used the local people to do so, including the Christians and Jews still living in the city. When the bedrock was exposed, they found two solid rock promontories within 300 feet of each other. The one to the south they named "as-Sakhra," and over as-Sakhra they built the memorial to Muhammad, the Dome of the Rock, the actual construction of which began in 688. You remember the numbers from the last chapter:

1290 Hebrew years (1271.5 Solar years) after 583BC is 688AD! 583 + 1271.34 = 688.66.

Over the other promontory – an unusually flat stone to the north and slightly west of as-Sakhra – a little, unimposing cupola was constructed they aptly named "The Dome of the Spirits," or "The Dome of the Tablets." Having no science of archaeology during those days, guess what?

The Moslems built the Dome of the Rock on the wrong rock![1]

Now I have no idea how you feel as you read that line, but I remember how I felt twenty two years ago when I first understood it. I sat at my desk, stunned for a moment, and then just leaned back and roared with laughter. I read the scriptural and archeological data again and again, praising God. The rock they built that dome on, As-Sakhra, has no historic or spiritual significance whatsoever. The Dome of the Rock is right in the middle of what was once the court of the Gentiles. Even ceremonially unwashed Canaanite slaves were allowed into the court of the

---

[1] According to Moslem tradition, As Sakhra is the rock from which Muhammad supposedly ascended into heaven. How spiritually appropriate it is that they built on the wrong rock. Muhammad is not just a little minor false prophet; he is probably THE false prophet of Rev 19:20! If he isn't, then what does it take to qualify?

Gentiles. You didn't have to be a priest, or a Levite, or even a Jew to be there.

The House of the Lord, which only the sons of Aaron could enter, stood over that little flat rock some 300+ feet north of where the Dome now stands. We know exactly where the temple stood because of holes drilled in the bedrock that are spaced on the sacred cubit. The sacred cubit could be used only in the temple itself, and these holes pinpoint the exact location of the House of the Lord.[1]

The *Kodesh Ha-Kodeshim*, the Holy of Holies, was directly over that little flat rock marked [X] on the drawing. Bathed in Shekinah Glory, that flat rock was the resting place of the Ark of the Covenant: "God's dwelling place, and the footstool of His feet, forever." It was exactly on an East-West line with the Golden Gate.[2] The very gate through which Jesus walked on His way to teach in the temple. Now, for the first time ever, we can discern the meaning of a baffling allegorical verse in Ezekiel:

> Eze 42:20 He measured it by the four sides: it had a wall round about, five hundred reeds long, and five hundred broad, to make a separation between the sanctuary and the profane place.

That spiritual wall of separation, probably guarded by holy angels, has stood on the temple mount for over 1300 years, and we haven't seen it. The Dome of the Rock is 300 feet to the South of the temple. That Moslem edifice is not now, and never has been, over the old temple site. The dome was, is, and shall be (as long as it stands) right in the middle of the Court of the Gentiles.

---

[1] The Hebrews had two units of measure for the cubit: the ordinary cubit of about 18 in., and a sacred cubit, "a cubit and a span" of about 21½ in. The sacred cubit was used only in temple construction.

[2] Temple Foundation Located, *Biblical Archaeology Review*, Mar. 1983.

THE 42 MONTHS

Isn't it wonderful to know that by permitting the temple's total destruction, God protected His Holy of Holies from the desecration of having a memorial to a false god, and the false prophet, built over it? Of more importance, if the Moslems had not built on the wrong rock, it would be impossible for this next quote to be fulfilled. Now look carefully at the language and see how perfectly it fits the situation on the temple mount today:

> Rev 11:2 But the court which is without the temple leave out, and measure it not; for it is given unto the Gentiles: and the holy city shall they tread under foot forty and two months.

"Leave out the court ... it has been given to the Gentiles!" The Dome of the Rock is in the court, and it is a Gentile structure. So we now have the location. Then we read that the city of Jerusalem itself would be under Gentile control for 42 months. Farfetched as it may sound, could those 42 months be months of days that should be looked at as years? It was day=years in the Old Testament, and there is no Scripture anywhere that does away with that interpretation, so let's at least try for a historic fit using day=years. When do they begin and when do they end? We need a historic setting.

On the 6th day of June, 1967, at the end of the Six-Day War, General Moshe Dayan and a tough, battle-hardened contingent of Israeli commandos stood before a wall of ancient stones. Their shoulders were shaking, and tears were streaming down their faces. They were at the Wailing Wall in East Jerusalem, that Holy Place from which they had been exiled so many centuries before. They were crying thanks unto God for restoring their ancient city to them. There they solemnly swore: "Never again shall we be driven from this place." For the first time in 2573 years the Jews were again in control of their Holy City. Could that touching moment be the historic end of, "and they [*the Gentiles*] will tread under foot the Holy City for 42 months?" 42 months x 30.44 gives us roughly 1278.5 days:[1]

1967AD - 1278.5 = 688.5AD ... the Dome of the Rock!

Bulls eye! In the 1290 days of Dan 12, the Lord took us from 583BC, and the abolition of sacrifices in Daniel's time, to 688AD and the Abomination that makes Desolate, the Dome of the Rock. Then in the 42 months, the Lord shows us the accuracy of that interpretation. He takes us from the restoration of Jerusalem in 1967, right back to 688, and the Dome of the Rock.

GRAPH NUMBER 7

42 Months of Rev 11:2

Rev 11:2 But the court which is without the temple leave out, and measure it not; for it is given unto the Gentiles: and the holy city shall they tread under foot forty *and* two months.

688AD
The Dome of the Rock

688AD
Jerusalem Freed

42 months = 1278.34 days. 1967AD - 1278.34 = 688.66AD

Note: Please study Rev 11:2 carefully. This interpretation fits Scripture and history too well to be ignored. "And the holy city shall they tread underfoot forty and two months." Forty-two months is 1278.34 days , and it is exactly 1278 years from the beginning of the construction of the Dome of the Rock until Jerusalem was again under Jewish control. Then, "Leave out the court ..." The Dome of the Rock is in the Court of the Gentiles, 300 feet south of the temple.

---

[1] A Solar year is 365.24 days. Dividing those days by the12 months in a year gives us a monthly duration of 30.44 days.

We come to 688, and that dome from both directions, right to the year. As a result, from the Lord's view, the central event to take place in Jerusalem during the time of the Gentiles was the building of the Abomination of Desolation on the footstool of His feet. And it is not just the numbers that work. Look at how this fits the very words of Scripture:

(1) "Sacrifices abolished."
(2) "Abomination set up."
(3) "Leave out the court."
(4) "Holy city tread under foot for 42 months."

This many factors coming together can't be just a numerical or verbal fluke, can they? Writing it off as coincidence is statistically unreasonable, and there are other fulfillments using the same yardstick still to come.

THE TIME OF JACOB'S TROUBLE

When God unlocks a book and opens our eyes, He does so in such a way that it cannot be reasonably refuted. Using the day=year principle again, God gives us proof upon proof:

> Rev 12:1-5 And there appeared a great wonder in heaven; a woman clothed with the sun, and the moon under her feet, and upon her head a crown of twelve stars: And she being with child cried, travailing in birth, and pained to be delivered. And there appeared another wonder in heaven; and behold a great red dragon, having seven heads and ten horns, and seven crowns upon his heads. And his tail drew the third part of the stars of heaven, and did cast them to the earth: and the dragon stood before the woman which was ready to be delivered, for to devour her child as soon as it was born. And she brought forth a man child, who was to rule all nations with a rod of iron: and her child was caught up unto God, and to his throne.

Who is this woman, and who is the man child? When we read His description, there is only one Person in all eternity who matches that portrait. Who will rule all nations with a rod of iron?[1] Who descended from Heaven, and who ascended up into it again?[2] Who now sits at the right hand of the throne of God?[3] None other than Jesus Christ the Righteous. That makes the woman Israel, and the 12 stars the 12 tribes. The dragon would then be Satan, who tried to defeat the Lord at the cross, and the fallen stars would be the fallen angels.[4]

> Rev 12:6 And the woman fled into the wilderness, where she hath a place prepared of God, that they should feed her there a thousand two hundred and threescore days.

During the Christian Era the Jews were dispersed into the nations.[5] For centuries the Jews have been hounded from country to country, made slaves of: were robbed, beaten, and murdered wholesale, as in Nazi Germany ... but never again. God has promised that never again would the Jews suffer anything like that holocaust in which 6,000,000 of the physical seed of Abraham were murdered:

> Jer 30:3-8 And these are the words that the LORD spake concerning Israel and concerning Judah. For thus saith the LORD; We have heard a voice of trembling, of fear, and not of peace. Ask ye now, and see whether a man doth travail with child? wherefore do I see every man with his hands on his loins, as a woman in travail, and all faces are turned into paleness? Alas! for that day is great, so that none is like it: it is even the time of Jacob's trouble, but he shall be saved out of it.

---

[1] Rev 19:15 And out of his mouth goeth a sharp sword, that with it he should smite the nations: and he shall rule them with a rod of iron.

[2] Eph 4:10 He that descended is the same also that ascended up far above all heavens, that he might fill all things.

[3] Col 3:1 If ye then be risen with Christ, seek those things which are above, where Christ sitteth on the right hand of God.

[4] Rev 1:20 tells us that the stars are the "aggelos" or messengers (Strong's No. G32). That same Greek word is also used in Rev 12:4. Aggelos, pronounced "anglos" is usually translated angels.

[5] The wilderness is the Gentile world, Eze 20:35.

A more moving account of the atrocities of the Nazi gas chambers would be hard to imagine. There, in the winter snow, stood line after line of Jewish men, naked, their hands in front of them to cover their nudity. Shivering bodies, numb with cold, beatings and starvation. Faces pale, they shuffled slowly into oblivion. As Your Son hung naked on the cross so long ago, so now it has happened unto Your people, Oh God.

But that is all in the past now. The time of Jacob's trouble is long over. The Lord has broken Satan's yoke from off their neck, and the Jews will never be in bondage again.

> Jer 30:7 For it shall come to pass in that day, saith the LORD of hosts, that I will break his yoke from off thy neck, and will burst thy bonds, and strangers shall no more serve themselves [*make slaves*] of him.

As of 1948, the Jews are no longer dispersed in the nations. On May 15th of that year, Israeli Prime Minister, David Ben-Gurion, stood on the floor of the Knesset and declared the nation of Israel to be a sovereign state. That is a historic fact nobody can dispute. As of 1948, the woman, Israel, is no longer in the wilderness, and since she isn't, Rev 12:6 is fulfilled.

According to Rev 12:6, the woman, Israel, would be in the wilderness 1260 days. Could this be years again? In this instance, the Lord gave us prophetic days straight out with no complicated mathematics.[1] Even a 2nd grader can figure this one out:

1948 - 1260 = 688 ... and the Dome of the Rock!

How come we couldn't see it sooner? God planned it that way, and even told us so. Remember in Dan 12:9, when the Lord stated that this book was sealed until the time of the end? Until the new nation of Israel and a freed Jerusalem became historic realities

---

[1] It is correct use the 365.24 solar year to interpret NT prophecies. In New Testament times, the Jews were under Roman rule and the 365.24 day Roman year was in common usage.

GRAPH NUMBER 8

The 1260 Days of Rev 12:6

Rev 12:6 And the woman fled into the wilderness, where she hath a place prepared of God, that they should feed her there a thousand two hundred *and* threescore days.

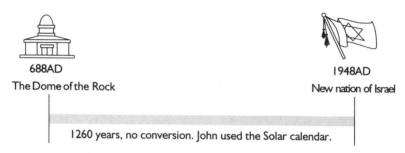

688AD

The Dome of the Rock

1948AD

New nation of Israel

1260 years, no conversion. John used the Solar calendar.

Note: Before 688AD, both Christians and Jews could freely worship in Jerusalem, and on the temple mount. They were not prophetically in the "wilderness" of the nations until the Moslems made it unsafe for them to worship in that city. That is why the 1260 days begin in 688AD.

(which BEGAN the time of the end) it was impossible to prove that Daniel's 1290 days were fulfilled by the Dome of the Rock.

Now you realize, according to the dispensationalists, that those prophetic "days" are supposed to be about either the first or the last half of the Great Seven-Year Tribulation, but obviously, that is not what they are about at all. They are about the Moslems, the Jews, Jerusalem, and the Holy Land. They are about the restoration of the people to whom God gave the land in the first place: the PHYSICAL descendants of Israel.

How can we deny the evidence of our own eyes? An Israeli flag, complete with the star of David, began to fly over the battlements of Jerusalem on the exact year the Lord predicted it would, and Jews by the millions have returned to the land. That's not guesswork theology, folks; it's reality.

Photo courtesy Biblical Archeology Review

We are filled with reverence when we realize that surrounding the now exposed bedrock under this little cupola, was the Holy of Holies of the temple of Solomon. On this rock once stood the Ark of the Covenant. When Solomon erected the temple in 966BC, this very space was filled with the Shekinah glory of God. The Ark was "lost" during Nebuchadnezzar's siege of Jerusalem. Jewish tradition states that the prophet Jeremiah took the Ark and the original tabernacle through a secret tunnel under Jerusalem and buried them on Mount Nebo. However, it now appears that the Table of Showbread, Altar of Incense and the Ark of the Covenant were buried in a cave under Golgotha.

Two Witnesses

CHAPTER 6

Can a woman forget her sucking child,
that she should not have compassion
on the son of her womb?
Yea, they may forget,
yet will I not forget thee.

ISA 49:15

AS already discussed, Revelation is not a mystery, but Jesus' solution of one (Rev 1:1). Consequently, we can't go to that book with our doctrines in place and expect to learn what Jesus may have there for us. The Two Witnesses of Rev 11:3-7 are good examples of why. Most believe these two witnesses to be a couple of Old Testament saints like Enoch and Elijah, but they might be someone else entirely:

> Rev 11:3 ... and I will grant authority to my two witnesses, and they will prophesy for twelve hundred and sixty days, clothed in sackcloth."

Taking the day-year principle of Eze 4:5-6 into consideration, those two witnesses would have to witness for 1260 years. No one in this age lives that long, so who can they be?

> Rev 11:4 These are the two olive trees, and the two candlesticks standing before the God of the earth.

Hummm ... olive trees and candlesticks. What can those figures mean? Unless the Lord's Two Witnesses are a pair of real elderly fruit-bearing olive trees and a couple of really ancient, oil-dripping candlesticks, then, like it or not, we are dealing with figurative language. So let's see if we can find biblical definitions for olive trees and candlesticks.

To sort these figures out we probably need to apply one of the rules of hermeneutics[1]. Now, hermeneutics is not a discipline we play games with to fit our doctrines. It is a sound study of how to interpret either the spoken word or a written document. Hermeneutics has some excellent, time-tested rules. Among them is the rule of "scriptural adjacency." That rule states: When you read something you don't understand, first study the surrounding text, then the chapter, then the book in which that chapter appears, then the testament that contains that book, and finally, relate the verse to the whole Bible. That is one of the rules, and it's a very good one. In other words ...

We don't go to the Old Testament for definitions of New Testament figures when there are New Testament definitions that fit perfectly! [2]

In Rev 11:4 quoted above, the Two Witnesses of the Christian Era are described as olive trees and candlesticks. To find the correct definition for those figures, we should find the closest contextual address which explains them. Lo and behold, right in Revelation we find candlesticks defined:

Rev 1:20 The mystery of the seven stars which thou sawest in My right hand, and the seven golden candlesticks. The seven stars are the angels of the seven churches: and the seven candlesticks which thou sawest are the seven churches.

---

[1] Hermeneutics is the science of interpretation, especially of the Scriptures. The branch of theology that deals with biblical exegesis.

[2] Candlesticks and olive trees are used figuratively in Zec 4, but the figures within that chapter were defined for us as things that existed during Zechariah's time (the Jewish leader Zerubbabel being one of them). So on the basis of the definitions in Zec 4, could Zerubbabel and "the two anointed ones" be the Two Witnesses of Rev 11? Not very likely since he died about 2500 years ago. We see no end-time reference to a personage like Zerubbabel in the New Testament, and furthermore Revelation does not call the two witnesses of the Christian Era "anointed ones." However, since Zechariah's two "anointed ones" are not clearly identified, they might possibly be an OT reference to the Two Witnesses in Revelation 11.

Right in Revelation 1, candlesticks are defined as churches. If candlesticks are churches in Rev 1, then guess what? Candlesticks are *still* churches in Rev 11. The only way they would not be Churches is if the Lord God Himself changed the symbolic meaning of that word somewhere between Rev 1:20 and Rev 11:4. No change of definition appears there (or anywhere else in Scripture for that matter) so the candlesticks of Rev 11:4 are churches. That interpretation is not the product of some clever theologian's overactive imagination. Candlesticks are churches because the Bible itself defines them as such.

So, if the seven candlesticks of Rev 1 are seven churches, what do you suppose the two candlesticks of Rev 11 might be? Why, two churches of course. But if the Two Witnesses are only two churches, which churches are they? Probably every denomination in the world would like to believe it is one of the Two Witnesses (with the rest of Christendom being heretics, of course), but God's churches of the Christian Era are far broader than man's sectarian restrictions, and the Olive Trees figure positively identifies who they are.

Still applying the principle of scriptural adjacency, we first try for a definition of olive trees in Revelation and then in the rest of the New Testament. Four times in the Old, and twice in the New, Israel is defined as an olive tree.[1] Old Testament verses are included in footnote, but we still don't use Old Testament

---

[1] Jer 11:16 The Lord called your name, "A green olive tree, beautiful in fruit and form;" With the noise of a great tumult He has kindled fire on it, And its branches are worthless.

Isa 17:6 Yet gleanings will be left in it like the shaking of an olive tree, Two or three olives on the topmost bough, Four or five on the branches of a fruitful tree, Declares the Lord, the God of Israel.

Isa 24:13 For thus it will be in the midst of the earth among the peoples, As the shaking of an olive tree, As the gleanings when the grape harvest is over.

Hos 14:6 His shoots will sprout, And his beauty will be like the olive tree, And his fragrance like Lebanon.

definitions to define New Testament figures when there are New Testament definitions that fit perfectly:

> Rom 11:17 And if some of the [*Jewish*] branches be broken off, and thou [*the Gentile church*], being a wild olive tree, wert grafted in among them, and with them partakest of the root and fatness of the olive tree.

> Rom 11:24 For if thou [*the Gentiles*] wert cut out of the olive tree which is wild by nature, and wert grafted contrary to nature into a good olive tree [*the Jews*]: how much more shall these [*the Jews*], which be the natural *branches,* be grafted into their own olive tree?

Revelation is a New Testament book, and a New Testament definition for olive trees appears in Romans 11. According to that whole chapter, the Gentile church is one olive tree, and the Jewish people are the other. As a result ...

One witness is the Jewish people
and the other witness is the Gentile church!

If we just accept the scriptural definitions for olive trees and candlesticks, we are not left with a lot of doctrinal options. Take a realistic look at history. The nation of Israel could not have maintained its identity through nineteen centuries of dispersion, under constant persecution, were it not for the protecting hand of the Lord our God. The Bible itself affirms it. Listen to what Scripture says:

> Jer 31:35-37 Thus saith the LORD, which giveth the sun for a light by day, *and* the ordinances of the moon and of the stars for a light by night, which divideth the sea when the waves thereof roar; The LORD of hosts *is* his name: If those ordinances depart from before me, saith the LORD, *then* the seed of Israel also shall cease from being a nation before me for ever. Thus saith the LORD; If heaven above can be measured, and the foundations of the earth searched out beneath, I will also cast off all the seed of Israel for all that they have done, saith the LORD.

Our eternal Heavenly Father has not forgotten those words. He stated right there that the children of Israel would be a *nation* before Him forever, so He has remembered His chosen people all along. The Lord's plans for the physical seed of Israel throughout all time, including the Christian Era, are recorded in too many Scriptures to ignore.[1]

Replacement theology[2] notwithstanding, from the multitude of verses cited in the footnote, it appears that the Lord never intended to forget the physical seed of Israel. Let me tell you how important that is. If the Jews could not trust the promises God made to them in the Old Testament, how can the Church trust the promises God made to us in the New? It's comforting to know, despite man's doctrines to the contrary, that our God is an absolutely Holy God who keeps His Word in eternity.

---

[1] Gen 17:7 speaks of an unconditional everlasting covenant with the physical seed of Abraham. Lev 26:44-45 shows that Israel's restoration was not to be conditional. Isa 11:11 speaks of a second restoration of the Jews. Isa 26:20-27:1 speaks of a final hiding of the children of Israel followed by Satan's complete judgment. Isa 27:12-13, in context with the above, speaks of a final re-gathering of Israel. Jer 30:4-8 speaks of the time of Jacob's trouble and future restoration. Jer 30:18-24 states that a restoration for the tents of Jacob will take place in the latter days, i.e. not the first restoration of 536BC. Jer 31:35-37 speaks of the permanent nation of Israel. Jer 33:24-26 is a definitive unconditional covenant with Jacob's descendants. Eze 16:60-63 speaks of an unconditional everlasting covenant with the Jews. Eze 37:1-28 speaks of an unconditional future restoration of Israel, followed closely by Armageddon in Exe 38-39. Hos 11:9-10 speaks of a future restoration of Israel from the West. Joe 3:1-3 predicts the restoration of Judah, followed by Armageddon. Amo 9:11-15 speaks of an Israel restored to the land. Zec 8:8 speaks of a post-exilic, unconditional restoration of the Jews to Jerusalem and the land. Zec 10 and 12 are more prophecies of a future restoration of the Jews. Zec 14 speaks of Armageddon, with the Jews in Jerusalem. Luk 21:24 speaks of a dispersion, the time of the Gentiles, and a restoration following. Rom 11:11 states that the Jews have not fallen so as to be lost. Rom 11:17 states that only some of the branches were broken off. Rom 11:17 states that the church was grafted in among the Jews. Rom 11:28 states that the gospel-age Jews are still elect. Rom 11:29 states that God's calling of the Jews is irrevocable. Rev 7:4-9 speaks of the 12 tribes of Israel in the Christian Era. Rev 12:1-6 speaks of Israel in the Christian Era. Rev 15:3 is a passage primarily about the Christian Era; there are two songs, one for the Jews, one for the Gentile church.

[2] Simply stated, Replacement Theology is the belief that the Church, as adopted Israel, has totally replaced the physical seed of Abraham and that God is completely finished with the Jews of the Christian Era. This view holds that during this era, the Church is all the Israel there is. The Scriptures cited in the preceding footnote, plus Rom 11:15, stand directly against such a doctrine.

Psa 33:11 The counsel of the LORD standeth for ever, the thoughts of his heart to all generations.

But if the Two Witnesses are two churches, when are they going to witness? If we stand by the day-year principle, they would have to witness for 1260 years:

Rev 11:3 And I will give *power* unto my two witnesses, and they shall prophesy a thousand two hundred *and* threescore days.

The time of the Two Witnesses cannot come after the time of the Gentiles because Jesus told us there would be only ONE generation following 1967: "This generation [*after the time of the Gentiles*] will not pass away until all things are fulfilled" (Luk 21:24, 32). A generation cannot be over 70 years (Psa 90:10), and is usually considered to be 40 years, so we have to look back in history for these 1260 years. The author could find only one 1260 year time period that had any spiritual significance at all during in the whole Christian Era:[1]

1948AD - 1260 = 688 AD and the Dome of the Rock!

And this fits history perfectly! As of 1948, the Jews are no longer witnessing in the nations. The Abomination that maketh Desolate was set up in 688, and the Jews were driven into the "wilderness" of the nations at that time.[2] Now, 1260 years later, there is a new autonomous nation of Israel, and the Jews are back in the Holy Land again. So the Jewish people are one of the Two Witnesses of the Christian Era.

---

[1] Since there have been Hebrew believers all the way back to Abraham's time, and the Church has existed since Pentecost, why do the 1260 days start in 688 AD? Before that date, both Jew and Christian were free to worship in Jerusalem, even on the temple mount itself. After 688 the Moslems persecuted the Christians and Jews and drove them out of the land. That is when the most final of all the dispersions of the Jews took place. By now we should begin to get the picture. God's Word is eternal, and regardless of what nation ruled in the Holy Land, that old temple site was always of inestimable importance to the Lord.

[2] Eze 20:35 "And I will bring you into the wilderness of the people," shows the Gentile nations to be the wilderness.

THE OTHER WITNESS

We can see 688 to 1948 as the time of Jewish witness, but what about the second witness, the Church? How can the church's time of witness be over since we are still here? Well, look at what has happened to the Church since 1948. Most Christian homes have a Bible, but few Christians still read them or continue to witness to the lost. The immorality, involvement in the occult and satanism in the western nations has mushroomed since 1948, and the church has done little to slow the decay. As a result of our apathy and questionable lifestyles that followed, much of the Gentile church has fallen into apostasy.

Most churches in this country are terminally ill, many have already fallen away, and Europe is far worse. Many are beyond reach, "the sin unto *spiritual* death" (1 Jo 5:16). Since our battle is really spiritual, one is inclined to wonder if the coming destruction of the visible Church may not be more spiritual than physical. If it is, we are frighteningly close to that hour:[1]

> Rev 11:7   And when they [*the Two Witnesses*] shall have finished their testimony, the beast that ascendeth out of the bottomless pit shall make war against them, and shall overcome them, and kill them.

One way or another, in the final hours of this age, the Two Witnesses are going to be destroyed. Read Rev 11:7 in the original Greek or in any translation you like. All predict the end of the visible Church. How can that be? Didn't Jesus promise that the

---

[1] The National Council of Churches (to which your own church might belong) joined the World Council of Churches in 1948. That organization has a declared goal of causing social change rather than teaching the gospel of Jesus Christ. That is what "Liberation Theology" is all about. It is reported that through them, millions of dollars from mainline denominational churches (your tithes included) have gone to buy guns to support various third-world insurgent "liberation fronts." As a result, it appears that the Gentile church has fallen into apostasy. As one indicator of church conditions, elders and deacons within mainline churches have become occultists and satanists or are into New Age.

gates of Hell would not prevail against His church? Yes, but the true Church that remains isn't all those big buildings out there, it's only a remnant now... a few hairs hidden in a hem of the Lord's garment (Eze 5:3).

For the first time since the invention of the printing press, books on astrology, satanism, and the occult are outselling the Bible. Truth has fallen in the street (Isa 59:14), and the consciences of our people have been seared as with a branding iron (1Ti 4:2). This will eventually lead to a worldwide rejection of the Bible and of the Lord. As the spiritual decay deepens, a ruthless and devastating evil will be unleashed upon this planet, and it will come with an intensity unknown since the flood. It has already begun.

GRAPH NUMBER 9

The Two Witnesses

Rev 11:3-4 And I will give *power* unto my two witnesses, and they shall prophesy a thousand two hundred *and* threescore days, clothed in sackcloth. These are the two olive trees, and the two Candlesticks standing before the God of the earth.

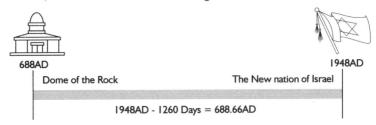

688AD   1948AD

Dome of the Rock   The New nation of Israel

1948AD - 1260 Days = 688.66AD

Note: Before 688, both Christians and Jews could freely worship in Jerusalem, and on the temple mount. They were not prophetically in the nations until the Moslems made it unsafe for them to worship in that city. That is why the time of the Two Witnesses began in 688.

What is a true Church to do when conditions become unbearable? Later in this book, you will read how we may become united with the faithful Jews, to stand with them in steadfast array against the enemies of the Lord:

> Isa 11:13-14 The envy also of Ephraim shall depart, and the adversaries of Judah shall be cut off: Ephraim shall not envy Judah, and Judah shall not vex Ephraim. But they shall fly upon the shoulders of the Philistines toward the west; they shall spoil them of the east together.

That verse may not seem applicable to a true Church today, but it's relevance will be explained in later chapters.

A NEWS BRIEF

Arutz Sheva Israel National Radio, 11/11/2001, 10:52am

> On the Hussan bypass road, near Beitar Illit, a very powerful bomb was discovered and safely detonated this morning. It contained a 120-mm mortar shell. Two mortar shells were fired at the Rafiach Crossing in southern Gaza in a pre-dawn attack this morning. There were no injuries.
>
> An Islamic Jihad terrorist was killed early this afternoon in an explosion at his place of work in Bethlehem. PLO sources say that the man probably suffered a "work accident" in the course of preparing explosives. They say they are continuing to check, however, whether he had been targeted by Israel.

Time, Times, & a Half
CHAPTER 7

But if ye turn unto me,
and keep my commandments, and do them;
though there were of you cast out
unto the uttermost part of the heaven,
yet will I gather them from thence,
and will bring them unto the place
that I have chosen to set my name there.

NEH 1:9

SO far, we have only studied prophetic days. In every instance we found them to be years. But day=years are not the only duration of prophetic time in the Bible. Twice in Daniel, and once in Revelation, there is the expression "time, times, and half a time." So how long is a time? Look at these times in Daniel:

> Dan 7:25   And he shall speak great words against the most High, and shall wear out the saints of the most High, and think to change times and laws: and they shall be given into his hand until a **time and times and the dividing of time**.

> Dan 12:7   And I heard the man clothed in linen, which was upon the waters of the river, when he held up his right hand and his left hand unto heaven, and sware by him that liveth for ever that it shall be for **a time, times, and an half**; and when he shall have accomplished to scatter the power of the holy people, all these things shall be finished.

Is a *time* a year like the day=years? One thing for sure, a *time* is not a year. Here is how we know. The Hebrew word for day is *yom*. The Hebrew and High Syriac words for *time* (as used in Dan

7:25 and 12:7) are *iddan* and *moadah*.[1] Surely, the Creator of the universe knows the difference between *iddan*, *moadah* and *yom*. Of course, and He gave us a *yom* for a year, not an *iddan* or a *moadah* for a year. So *iddan* (time), and *moadah* (time), must mean something else. Lets call them time durations "X."

And what about the cryptic way in which those words were used, "time, times, and the dividing of a time?" How many "times" do we have there? As is true of English, Hebrew is full of idiomatic language. For instance, the Hebrew idiom "cut off" means to kill. "Ate the pieces of" means to bring malicious accusations against, and so on. Is "time, times, and the dividing of a time" also an idiom? Let's see if there is Scripture to support that hypothesis:

> Job 33:14 For God speaketh once, yea twice, yet man perceiveth it not.
> Job 40:5 Once have I spoken; but I will not answer: yea, twice; but I will proceed no further.
> Psa 62:11 God hath spoken once; twice have I heard this; that power belongeth unto God.

In the above, *once* is one, and *twice* is only one more, for a total of two: $1+1=2$. A singular *one* followed by a plural *twice* is only two. In the same way, a singular *time* followed by a plural *times* might be only two. Only two! The words are different, but the idiomatic form is the same. If the Lord had said, "time, yea times" we might have seen it instantly.

Now let's employ the same idiomatic language to interpret time, times, and half a time. *Time* = one; *times* = one more, for a total of two times. Add a *half a time* and we have two and a half

---

[1] DAY= H3117. yowm, yome: from an unused root mean. to be hot; a day (as the warm hours), whether lit. (from sunrise to sunset, or from one sunset to the next. TIME= H5732. 'iddan, (Chaldean), id-dawn': from a root corresponding. to that of H5708; a set time. TIME= H4150. mow'ed, mo-ade'; or mo'ed mo-ade'; or (feminine) mow'adah (H2 Chron. 8 :13), mo-aw-daw': from H3259; prop. an appointment, i.e. a fixed time or season.

times, or $1+1+\frac{1}{2}=2\frac{1}{2}$.[1] That is pretty simple, isn't it? So why have people been saying that "time, times, and half a time" are three and a half years? Who knows? Probably because it fits the *Seven-Year* tribulation scheme. However, Hebrew scholars have told me their grammar does not support $3\frac{1}{2}$ times as the correct translation for that idiom.

All right, so "time, times, and half a time" are two and a half times. But if a time isn't a year, how long is it? Daniel understood day=years, but he didn't understand *time*. Why? Because day=years were defined for him in Old Testament scriptures while time was not. In fact, *time* was not defined until late in the New Testament epistles:

> 2Pe 3:8 But, beloved, be not ignorant of this one thing, that one day [*Greek word, hemera*] is with the Lord as a thousand years, and a thousand years as one day.

On the surface that sure doesn't look like much of a definition for time, does it? It certainly doesn't work in English. But something is wrong here. God has already given us the definition for day. He gave us a day for a year. Is the Lord changing His definition of prophetic days here? Not at all. We can prove that the correct interpretation for prophetic days is still years by the 42 months and 1260 days of Revelation that we just studied.

What we have here is an "X with the Lord is as a thousand years, and a thousand years is as an X." So how do we solve for "X"? By doing a word study in Greek, which was the original language of the New Testament. The Greek word translated "day" in 2Pe 3:8 is *hemera*, ($\dot{\eta}\mu\acute{\epsilon}\rho\alpha$).[2] Hemera is an ambiguous word

---

[1] Sorry about this $1+1$ stuff. I know I am getting down on the kindergarten level, but this seems the easiest way to explain the concept.

[2] Strong's No. G2520. hemera, hay-mer'-ah: feminine. (with G5610 implied) of a der. of hemai (to sit; akin to the base of G1476) several days were usually reckoned by the Jews as inclusive of the parts of both extremes; fig. a period (always defined more or less clearly by the context): age, + always, forever, judgment, (day) time, while, years.

sometimes translated: period, moment, season, year, and, guess what ... *Time*. So what is the correct translation here? In Greek, context often determines translation, but in the above verse, the correct translation cannot be established with certainty because context does not suggest the correct concept. Understandably, translators went with "day," which is the most common usage, but that may not be correct. *Hemera* is translated *time* in four verses in the KJV, and twelve verses in the NASB. So *time* is a very acceptable translation. Is it possible that duration "X" is a thousand years?

If *time* is a thousand years, and we have 2½ of them, then "time, times, and half times" could be 2500 years. Thus far, we have only a supposition. But that is all we had for day=years until we started plugging them into history. Let's see if there is an exact 2500 year historic fit that fulfills the Bible's description of these *times* right to the year.

After Nebuchadnezzar of Babylon died in 562BC, each of his three sons ruled for a couple of years.[1] The kingdom was very unstable. Though the archives don't tell us a lot about it, reading about those Middle Eastern empires from secular sources gives us a picture of what must have been going on there. King Labashi-Marduk was murdered as a mere child. Daniel must have been walking on eggs to avoid the plots and political intrigue in the Babylonian court. Many of his fellow rulers in Babylon hated him and some even plotted his death (Dan 6:4-13). However, the Lord protected Daniel in that harrowing environment.

Then in 555BC, a nephew of Nebuchadnezzar named Nabonidus seized the throne. He proved to be a very able ruler. However, he couldn't stomach the Babylonian court life, so three years later, in 552, he chose a close relative, Belshazzar, to rule

---

[1] Nebuchadnezzar was succeeded by his eldest son Awel-Marduk – the Evil-Merodach of 2 Kings 25:27-30 (561-560BC). Awel-Marduk was followed by Neriglissar (560-558 BC), who was succeeded by Labashi-Marduk (557BC).

the empire for him. Then Nabonidus spent the rest of his life wandering around Arabia, doing archeological digs and writing lots of poetry.[1]

During these turbulent times, the Lord gave Daniel the vision of four great beasts coming up out of the sea.[2] Scripture tells us when this was, right to the year, "In the 1st year of Belshazzar" (Dan 7:1). In pictorial language, the vision then describes the four great kingdoms that were to rule in the Holy Land during the time of the Gentiles. At the end of that prophecy, the Lord tells Daniel about *times*:

> Dan 7:25 And he shall speak great words against the Most High and shall wear out the saints of the most High, and think to change times and laws: and they shall be given into his hand until a time and times and the dividing of time.

Sometimes our doctrines get messed up because we don't think about who the Lord is speaking to, or when. In this instance, the Lord is speaking to Daniel in 552BC.

So in Daniel's day, who spoke out against God? Then, as now, Satan speaks out against God. Who were the saints in Daniel's time? The Jews, of course. So from 552BC, when this prophecy was given, the Lord is telling Daniel that the Jews would be under satanically controlled Gentile powers for two and a half times, or possibly 2500 years. That the Holy Land would be ruled by Gentile strangers far into the future. Now let's run that up and down the framework of history and see what it fits. Since the definition for time was given in the New Testament, we don't even need to

---

[1] To date, there is no direct archeological evidence for 552BC being the 1st year of the Belshazzar's regency. However, that date can be supported by correlating evidence about the reign of Nabonidus. John Walvoord, *The Key to Prophetic Revelation* (Chicago, Moody Press, 1971) p. 115 accepts a 553BC Belshazzar dating, and most authorities recognize a one to three year ambiguity in Old Testament dating.

[2] The sea is the peoples of the Earth (Rev 17:15): "The waters which thou sawest ... are peoples, and multitudes, and nations, and tongues."

convert from Hebrew to solar years to fit our calendar. A simple subtraction will do just fine:

2500 - 552BC = 1948AD, and new Israel!

Just a lucky hit? If that is not the correct interpretation, then it has to be one of the most remarkable coincidences in all of recorded history. It fits Scripture and history, right to the year. But remarkable as that fulfillment of prophecy may be, we would still have only a theory if it was the only 2500 year *time* period that fit antiquity.

GRAPH NUMBER 10

1ˢᵗ **Time, Times & Half a Time**

Dan 7:25 And he shall speak *great* words against the most High, and shall wear out the saints of the most High, and think to change times and laws: and they shall be given into his hand until a time and times and the dividing of time.

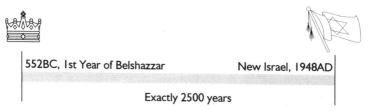

| 552BC, 1st Year of Belshazzar | New Israel, 1948AD |

Exactly 2500 years

God is so kind. When He takes the blinders off, He gives enough proof for us to know for sure that we are headed in the right direction. At the end of Daniel's prophetic ministry, God gave him another vision containing *times*. This prophecy also includes the 1290 days which led us to understand that the Dome of the Rock is the Abomination that makes Desolate. This vision may be dated to the third year of Cyrus the Persian, or 533BC:

> Dan 10:1 In the third year of Cyrus king of Persia a thing was revealed unto Daniel, whose name was called Belteshazzar .

Daniel was now a very old man. He knew he was going to go to be with the Lord soon. The temple mount had been abandoned and sacrifices abolished during his own lifetime. He knew that an Abomination of Desolation was going to stand on that beloved temple mount in less than 1300 years. Would the Jews ever control Jerusalem again? Of course. Many Old Testament Scriptures told him so. But when? The Lord told him that as well, right to the year, but then hid it so that no one would know when that time would be, until it happened:

> Dan 12:7 And I heard the man clothed in linen, which was upon the waters of the river, when he held up his right hand and his left hand unto heaven, and sware by him that liveth for ever that it shall be for a time, times, and half; and when he shall have accomplished to scatter the power of the holy people, all these things shall be finished.

Three years earlier, Cyrus had given a decree that would permit the Jews to return to their homeland. They had begun their trek back to the Holy land, and soon they would begin to build the 2nd temple. That temple stood until 70AD, when the Jews were driven from the land again. But God knew the end of this second dispersion, too. He knew that at the end of it, the Jews would return to the Holy Land one more time and again control Jerusalem. When was the vision given? In 533BC, the third year of Cyrus. So this "time, times, and half a time" should begin in the third year of Cyrus:

2500 - 533BC = 1967AD
Jerusalem freed of Gentile control!

GRAPH NUMBER 11

2nd Time, Times & Half a Time

Dan 12:7 And ... he held up his right hand and his left hand unto heaven, and sware by him that liveth for ever that *it shall be* for a time, times, and an half; and when he shall have accomplished to scatter the power of the holy people, all these *things* shall be finished.

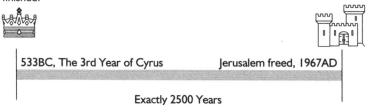

533BC, The 3rd Year of Cyrus   Jerusalem freed, 1967AD

Exactly 2500 Years

Note: When the Jews again took control of Jerusalem in 1967, the "scattering of the power of the holy people" was over. Daniel was a prophet to the time of the Gentiles. Daniel's prophecies were, in the main, fulfilled in 1967AD. This does not include the last half of Dan 8, which directly states that it is a vision of "the ultimate time of the end."

The Lord even worded the last phrase of that prophecy in such a way that it would be difficult to miss His intent: "... and when he shall have accomplished to scatter [*or shatter, NASB*] the power of the holy people, all these things shall be finished." As of 1967AD, His holy people, the Jews, were no longer scattered among the Gentiles. They have their nation again, and their power is shattered no longer.

A SEASON AND A TIME

There is a third *time* in Daniel that proves a prophetic *"time"* to be a thousand years. The four beasts of Daniel 7 are understood to be the great Gentile empires that would rule in the Holy Land during the time of the Gentiles. The first three beasts were Babylon, Medo-Persia and Greece. The fourth beast, Rome, fell in 476AD (*more on these empires in a later chapter*). The Moslems came on the scene soon after Rome fell, but the Moslems were not granted world dominion like the empires that came before them; however, the Lord did permit the Islamic states to rule in the Holy Land for a "season and a time":

> Dan 7:11-12 I beheld *even* till the [*4th*] beast [*Rome*] was slain, and his body destroyed, and given to the burning flame. As concerning the rest of the beasts [*the Islamic nations of the Middle East*], they had their dominion taken away: yet their lives [*in the holy Land*] were prolonged for a season and time.

If time is 1000 years and there are four seasons, then a season would be $1/4^{th}$ of a time, or 250 years. $1000+250=1250$. Remembering that a season is not an exact number and could fluctuate a week or two either way, this "season and time" fits history well, indeed.

> *New Israel became a nation a "Season and Time,"*
> *(1260 years) after the Dome of the Rock was built.*

We have seen three examples, from Daniel alone, of *time* fitting history, when *time* is understood to be a thousand years. Consequently, it is unrealistic to hold that prophetic *times* mean anything else. Brethren, I'll accept time=1000 years as a coincidence once, but not three times. These solutions span thousands of years, from historic events that took place in antiquity to historic events that have taken place in our own lifetimes. That is a statistical impossibility, so we no longer have just a theory; we have a sound biblical and historically supportable doctrine[1].

---

[1] There is a further message in Dan 12:7: "all these things shall be finished" shows that all events predicted in Daniel's last vision, including "Michael standing up," were fulfilled by 1967. This brings to an end the contention that Dan 11:36-45 is about some period in our future or about a coming antichrist. These verses are all fulfilled.

GRAPH NUMBER 12

A Season and a Time

Dan 7:11 I beheld then because of the voice of the great words which the horn spake: I beheld even till the beast [Rome] was slain, and his body destroyed, and given to the burning flame.

Dan 7:12 As **concerning the rest of the beasts** [the Islamic Nations of the Middle East], they had their dominion taken away: yet their lives were prolonged for a season and time.

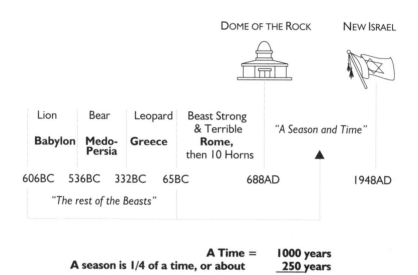

DOME OF THE ROCK				NEW ISRAEL
Lion	Bear	Leopard	Beast Strong & Terrible	"A Season and Time"
Babylon	**Medo-Persia**	**Greece**	**Rome,** then 10 Horns	▲
606BC	536BC	332BC 65BC	688AD	1948AD

"The rest of the Beasts"

A Time =	**1000 years**
A season is 1/4 of a time, or about	**250 years**
Total =	**1250 years**

NOTE: A season is generally considered to be a fourth of a year, but it is an indefinite time that can vary by a week or so. Consequently, this "season and a time" from the Dome of the Rock to new Israel is a dead hit, and it proves from Daniel itself that a prophetic "time" should be understood to be 1000 years.

In *times* and day=years, we have a solid empirical argument, a prophetic jigsaw puzzle in which all the pieces interlock with each other. We can argue about the placement, color, or shape of any one piece, but when the whole puzzle is put together, we can stand back and view a completed picture. It's not so easy to discredit a prophetic picture in which all the elements fit perfectly.

If it is not of God, it will crumble back into its original pieces on its own; however, if it is of God, it will remain and flourish, no matter who comes against it (Act 5:35-39).

These day=year and *time* prophecies are truly remarkable. They show the sovereignty of a timeless God over the affairs of men in a way that is difficult to dispute, and they do so over eons of time. Despite the best efforts of the enemy and the complexity of 2500 years of history, God not only foreknew what was going to happen in the Holy Land, but He managed history in such a way that what the Bible prophesied did take place, right to the year, at His chosen location, in His chosen time. Astounding.

NEWS BRIEF

Arutz Sheva Israel National Radio, 11/20/2001, 11:18am

> The three Shavei Shomron residents who were wounded in yesterday's attempted terrorist murder outside their community are still hospitalized. Shimrit Haibi, 17, is in moderate-to-serious condition, her father Ya'ir is listed in moderate condition, and Rabbi Yehoshua Shmidt was lightly hurt. The three were travelling in a taxi when they were hit by several rounds of fire. Rabbi Shmidt told Arutz-7 today that though two bullets passed through his kippah (skullcap), "G-d protects us, and my head was only grazed."

Mounting Evidence
CHAPTER 8

He hath remembered his covenant forever,

the word which he commanded

to a thousand generations.

PSA 105:8

SO far, you have read some almost unbelievable Bible prophecies, many of which have come to pass right in our own generation. All were about Jerusalem, the Jewish people, the Holy Land or Islam. All were timed prophecies and all were fulfilled right to the year. Let's review those prophecies for a moment:

1. The 1290 days of Dan 12:11 fulfilled in 688AD by the construction of the Moslem Dome of the Rock.
2. The 42 months of Rev 11:2 fulfilled in 1967AD by the freeing of Jerusalem from Gentile control.
3. The 1260 Days of Rev 11:3 fulfilled in 1948AD by the Jewish people returning to their homeland.
4. The 1260 days of Rev 12:5 fulfilled in 1948AD by the establishment of the new nation of Israel.
5. The Time, Times and Half Time of Dan 7:25 fulfilled in 1948AD by the new nation of Israel.
6. The Time, Times and Half Time of Dan 12:7 fulfilled in 1967AD by the freeing of Jerusalem.
7. The Season and Time of Dan 7:12 fulfilled in 1948AD when Gentiles lost control of the Holy Land.

It is a statistical impossibility for all the above prophecies to exactly fit Scripture and history to the year, as they do, unless this is the correct interpretation; and my, what doors of understanding those prophecies open for us. Looking back at the rest of the Bible through the doctrinal filter the "Great Detective" has given us in Revelation, we now know that the time of the Gentiles is over.

Since we can identify the Two Witnesses, we also know that God has not forgotten His chosen people, the Jews. We further know that the Abomination of Desolation is not an antichrist in our future, but a building that has stood on Mount Moriah for over 1300 years. In addition, since prophecies throughout Revelation have already been fulfilled, it appears that the book is not about events in some future tribulation period, but about happenings within our own Christian Era. These fulfillments of prophecy are real, folks, whether we are ready for them or not, and they strongly impact the rest of our end-time doctrines.

All those prophecies were thought to be about a Seven Year Great Tribulation, but they aren't! 688, 1948 and 1967 were pivotal years, indeed. What follows now are the conclusions to which I was inexorably driven as I built logically on the prophetic importance of the new nation of Israel and Islam as shown through the day=years and times. If we stand behind Revelation, as we now can, and look back at the rest of the Bible through the filter of what that book has taught us, a totally new doctrinal picture appears. A picture that is very hard to believe.

The historic fulfillment of Daniel's *times* enables us to understand Revelation's *times*, and Revelation's *times* show us what happened to the ten tribes of northern Israel after Shalmaneser of Assyria dispersed them into Mesopotamia in 725-722BC, and knowing what happened to those ten tribes is of importance to us. Who and where are they? That story appears to be hidden in the native religions of isolated tribes like the Karen, Yalu, Rengma, and Lahu.

One More Time

CHAPTER 9

They shall come with weeping,
and with supplications will I lead them:
I will cause them to walk
by the rivers of waters in a straight way,
wherein they shall not stumble:
for I am a father to Israel,
and Ephraim is my firstborn.

JER 31:9

DEEP in the mountainous interior of Irian Jaya, formerly Dutch New Guinea, there lives a tribe of natives called the Yalu. They were one of the most isolated peoples on the face of the earth yet they had a very formalized blood sacrificial system. They had a law of Ten Commandments called the *wene malalek* and a holy ground called an *osuwa*. That *osuwa* was surrounded by a stone wall. Any man not consecrated to the spirits of *kembu*, or any woman who trespassed on that ground, would be killed. Within the *osuwa* was a sacred building called the *kembu-vam*. It had two rooms, an outer room where the priests of *kembu* held ceremonies, and an inner room which held the sacred stone. The stone was never allowed to be moved by one man, but had to be carried by four men at its four corners. Pigs were slaughtered and roasted in the court outside the *kembu-vam*, and priests, with awesome ceremony, took pig fat into that holiest of rooms and anointed the sacred stone.[1]

---

[1] A more detailed account of the Yalu folk religion may be found in Don Richardson's *Lords of the Earth* (Ventura, CA Regal Books, 1977) pp. 76-80.

Though unbelievably corrupted, the parallels of the Yalu folk religion to the Levitical code are so inescapable that one has to ask: Where did they get all that?

In Burma, there was a tribe of people called the Karen who worshiped the God Y'wa. Their prophets declared that they once possessed a book of the law but had lost it many centuries before. Sacred songs passed down from generation to generation, reminded them of their lost law:

> *Omnipotent is Y'wa; Him have we not believed.*
> *Y'wa created men anciently.*
> *He has a perfect knowledge of all things.*
> *Y'wa created men at the beginning.*
> *The earth is the treading place for the feet of Y'wa.*
> *And heaven is the place where He sits.*
> *He sees all things and we are manifest to Him.*
>
> *Y'wa formed the earth originally.*
> *He appointed food and drink.*
> *He appointed the "fruit of trial."*
> *Mu-kaw-lee deceived two persons.*
> *He causes them to eat of the fruit of the tree of trial.*
> *They obeyed not; they believed not Y'wa ...*
> *They became subject to sickness, aging and death ...*
>
> *O children and grandchildren,*
> *If we repent of our sins,*
> *And cease to do evil - restraining our passions -*
> *And pray to Y'wa. He will have mercy upon us again.*
> *If Y'wa does not have mercy on us, there is no other one*
> *who can.*
> *He who saves us is the only one - Y'wa.*
> *O Children and grandchildren! Pray to Y'wa constantly.*
> *By day and by night.*[1]

---

[1] Don Richardson, *Eternity in Their Hearts* (Ventura, CA, Regal Books, 1981) pp.77-79, cites from *The Gospel in Burma,* Wylie, p. 6, and *The Karen Apostle,* Mason, p. 97-99.

Y'wa is just too close to Yahweh (the Hebrew name for God) to be coincidental. And what about the "fruit of trial" and prayer? Those traditions do not appear to be founded in the New Testament Gospel, but upon a knowledge of the Old Testament. Again we have to ask: Where did they get all that?

The Lahu of northern Burma had a tradition that *Gui'Sha*, the Creator of all things, had given their forefathers His law written on rice cakes. The Rengma tribe in India believed that the Supreme Being gave His words to their forefathers written on animal skins *(which, by the way, is what the Mosaic law was written on)*. But according to their traditions, the forefathers of the Rengma people had been careless with the skins and dogs had eaten them.[1]

These examples are not unique. The native religions of almost every isolated people on earth contain haunting memories, in varying detail, of an earlier knowledge of the true God, or of His Law. So, once again we ask; where did all this knowledge come from? To find out, we may need to go back again into the history of the children of Israel ...

Jacob, named Israel by the Lord, was Abraham's grandson. Jacob had twelve sons, among whom was Joseph, and those twelve men became the fathers of the twelve tribes of the nation of Israel. After the death of Jacob, Israel's twelve tribes remained in Egypt for 430 years. They fled Egypt in 1446BC, and were in the wilderness for another 40 years. After Joshua's conquest of Canaan, they lived in the Promised Land, under judges, for another 300 years. Then, during the judgeship of Samuel, the people demanded to have a king.

God first gave them Saul, then David, and with David began the line of kings through which Jesus would be born. But the kingdom remained unified for only two generations. If you read the account carefully, it appears that Solomon, the wisest man who

---

[1] Ibid pp. 85-91

ever lived, had a son who was truly inept. Rehoboam's decision to raise taxes caused a revolt, so during his reign the Davidic kingdom divided. God separated Judah and Benjamin from the ten northern tribes, and the twelve tribes became two separate nations: Israel in the North, and Judah in the South. Jerusalem remained the capital of Judah while Samaria became the capital of Israel.

Northern Israel remained in continual rebellion to the Lord, putting it in conflict with Judah and the nations around them. Finally, in 748BC, Tiglath-pileser of Assyria made northern Israel a vassal state and took captives off to Assyria. In 725BC, Shalmaneser began a major deportation of Israel, and put Samaria under siege. Samaria itself fell in 722BC and what was left of the nation of Israel was taken captive and relocated near the Caspian Sea (north of what is now Iran) and they were never heard from again. This happened just as Moses prophesied it would:

> Neh 1:8 Remember, I beseech thee, the word that thou commandedst thy servant Moses, saying, *If* ye transgress, I will scatter you abroad among the nations:

Why did God ever allow this to happen? Were the Israelites not part of God's chosen people? Didn't the everlasting covenant God made with Abraham include the ten tribes? The prophet Isaiah saw what was going on around him and lamented:

> Isa 63:17 O LORD, why hast thou made us to err from thy ways, *and* hardened our heart from thy fear? Return for thy servants' sake, the tribes of thine inheritance.

The fall of northern Israel was not just an unfortunate accident in history. It was an integral part of God's eternal plan, and the Lord told His people about it in advance.

Hosea was placed in Israel just before its fall, and he alone details the future of the ten tribes after their dispersion among the Gentile nations. Hosea prophesied from about 750-722BC and he prepares God's people for the calamity that is about to befall them. Read the prophet carefully, and you will see that the destruction of Israel and Samaria is fixed. It is going to fall to Assyria, no matter what. Hosea is not a call to repentance to save the northern kingdom. Instead, the prophet is describing the Lord's plan for the ten northern tribes *after* they disappeared.

GRAPH NUMBER 13

History of the Ten Tribes

Lev 26:32-33 And I will bring the land into desolation: and your enemies which dwell therein shall be astonished at it. And I will scatter you among the heathen, and will draw out a sword after you: and your land shall be desolate, and your cities waste.

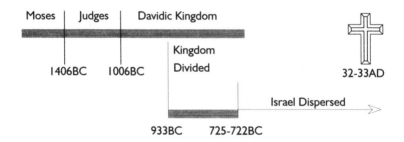

In the verse below, we begin to see the everlasting love our Heavenly Father has for His wayward Israelites. While they were figuring out ways to rebel against Him, God was putting a long-term plan in motion to save them: a plan spanning thousands of years. The following verse is in that setting. Israel is about to go into captivity when God tells them:

Hos 1:10 Yet the number of the children of Israel shall be as the sand of the sea, which cannot be measured nor numbered; and it shall come to pass, that in the place where it was said unto them, Ye are not my people, there it shall be said unto them, Ye are the sons of the living God.

That is a paradoxical Scripture is it not? Note the tense of the verb, "shall be." Shall be is future to when it was written. Israel is about to go into captivity never to be heard from again, and the Lord tells them that they are going to be numerous beyond count.

Furthermore, He tells them that no one will know they are His Israelites. Nonetheless, they will be called the sons of God. Isn't that mystifying?

> Hos 2:19-20 And I will betroth thee unto me for ever ... I will even betroth thee unto me ... and thou shalt know the LORD.

The Lord then declares that this lost and scattered people will be His bride, a bride whether they know it or not. Impossible from man's standpoint, nevertheless, an accomplished fact from God's. But there is more. If we picture in our minds how seed was sown in the old days, we can also understand this unique Old Testament figure of the sower:

> Hos 2:23 And I will sow her [Israel] unto me in the earth; and I will have mercy upon her that had not obtained mercy; and I will say to them which were not my people, Thou art my people; and they shall say, Thou art my God.

Taking from his bag of grain, an ancient farmer would cast seed evenly over every square foot of his field with a side-wise motion of his arm. That is what the Lord did with Israel. He scattered Israelites all over His great field, the earth, from South Africa to China. Oh my, can you see it? God scattered the seed of Israel over the whole world, from Terra del Fuego to the tip of Siberia.

Descendants of the lost tribes of Israel are everywhere, and God did not disperse them to lose them. In spite of their scattering, the Lord declared that He would have mercy on them. Here, at the beginning of the 21st century, it is only a hundred generations from when God made an everlasting covenant with Abraham. Since the very hairs of our heads are numbered, surely the Lord has no trouble remembering every one of Israel's descendants. The prophet Amos also spoke of this continuing covenant with a dispersed Israel, but in figurative language:

Amo 9:9 For, lo, I will command, and I will sift the house of Israel among all nations, like as *corn* is sifted in a sieve, yet shall not the least grain fall upon the earth.

Can we hear that? "Yet shall not the least grain fall upon the earth?" The Creator of the universe was going to save his wayward Israelites. But not only them. God didn't have just a little local plan to deal with a few Israelites. The Lord saw and planned the history of the whole world and its inhabitants in eternity and He is very good. Everything God does is good. So it is reasonable to believe that the Lord scattered the ten tribes of Israel abroad for a good reason, and not just as judgment upon His people. To see why Israel was dispersed, we need to stand outside our 21st century mind-set and look back on Earth's 6000 years of recorded history from the standpoint of God's overall plan.

Earlier in this chapter we saw how bits of the true faith were spread among the primitive peoples of the world.[1] Apostate as northern Israel became, it is scripturally provable that there were still men within it who retained a knowledge of God and of His law (2 Ki 17:26-28). Taking a broad view of history, it appears that 700 years before Jesus was born, the Lord may have spread the children of Israel over the whole earth for the express purpose of sharing the knowledge of the true God with the Gentile nations. To prepare the hearts of the people of the world for the coming of Messiah and the preaching of the Gospel. Now we can see a literal fulfillment of a verse that is usually spiritualized:

---

[1] Because parallels to prominent historic Israelite figures like Abraham, Moses, and David do not appear in most native religions, Don Richardson (author of *Eternity in their Hearts, Peace Child* and *Lords of the Earth*) questions whether these religions originally sprang from Hebrew roots. But the beliefs of these primitive peoples were passed down by oral tradition over the 2700 years that Israel has been dispersed. During that length of time, almost any amount of corruption or omission could have taken place. The importance of their great historic figures would have lessened as the memory of their deeds was lost in antiquity. If a culture barely remembers that it once had a "lost book," it seems unlikely that it would remember who wrote it, or what it contained.

Rom 11:25-26 Blindness in part is happened to Israel, until the fulness of the Gentiles be come in. **And thus all Israel shall be saved**.

What does that verse say? That Gentiles must come to the Lord for all Israel to be saved. But when the Gentiles do turn to Jesus, *ALL Israel shall be saved!* Do you see what that verse could mean if taken literally? Despite the dispersion of the ten northern tribes, it could mean that God intended to save the Israelites all along, and in the Christian Era there is only one way He would do so: by leading them to a knowledge of His Son. Everyone in the Church may not be a direct descendant of Jacob, but from Amos 9:9 and the other verses we have read, it is reasonable to conclude that the dispersed descendants of Israel are saved and in the Church.

No matter what the color of your skin, or where you are on this planet, if you have come to the Lord with a humble heart it is very possible that you are a physical descendant of one of the ten tribes of Israel, and as such you could be the physical brother or sister of every other believer on Earth. Greetings, then, my brother or sister, in the name of our Lord and Savior, Jesus Christ.

EPHRAIM, WHERE ARE YOU?

Now we have discussed all Israel, but what happened to the tribe of Ephraim? Joseph had two sons, Manasseh and Ephraim. Our historic setting for the following quote is with them, in Egypt, at Israel's bedside 3700 years ago. The great seven-year famine is long past. Jacob is old and full of years. He is almost blind, and now he is about to die.

Jacob (Israel) called his twelve children around him to give them his final blessing. Joseph and his two sons were ushered in first. Joseph herding his boys before him, just as any parent would do when he wants you to notice his children:

Gen 48:13 And Joseph took them both, Ephraim in his right hand toward Israel's left hand, and Manasseh in his left hand toward Israel's right hand, and brought them near unto him. 14-16 And Israel stretched out his right hand, and laid it upon Ephraim's head, who was the younger, and his left hand upon Manasseh's head, guiding his hands wittingly; for Manasseh was the firstborn. And he blessed Joseph, and said, God, before whom my fathers Abraham and Isaac did walk, the God which fed me all my life long unto this day, The Angel which redeemed me from all evil, bless the lads; and let my name be named on them, and the name of my fathers Abraham and Isaac; and let them grow into a multitude in the midst of the earth. 17-18 And when Joseph saw that his father laid his right hand upon the head of Ephraim, it displeased him: and he held up his father's hand, to remove it from Ephraim's head unto Manasseh's head. And Joseph said unto his father, Not so, my father: for this is the firstborn; put thy right hand upon his head. 19 And his father refused, and said, I know it, my son, I know it: he also shall become a people, and he also shall be great: but truly his younger brother shall be greater than he, and **his seed shall become a multitude of nations**.

So the half tribe of Manasseh would become a great people, but further into the future, the half tribe of Ephraim would become a multitude of nations. Ephraim never did become a multitude of nations in Old Testament times, so if they didn't do so *before* they were taken captive, they would have do so *after* they were absorbed into the Gentile world. Obviously, the tribe of Ephraim is not out there claiming to be Israel, so they must not even know who they are themselves. Where has the Lord hidden them, and can it be proven biblically?

Hos 11:8-9 How shall I give thee up, Ephraim? how shall I deliver thee, Israel Mine heart is turned within me, my repentings are kindled together ... I will not execute the fierceness of mine anger, I will not return to destroy Ephraim: for I am God, and not man; the Holy One in the midst of thee.

As the warrior tribe, Ephraim was the most powerful house in Israel. In fact, that tribe was so influential that Ephraim's name was sometimes used in reference to all ten tribes. But when the Lord tells us He will not give Israel up, He does make a special reference to Ephraim, so Ephraim might have a special prophetic significance.

> Hos 11:10 ... then the children [*of Ephraim*] shall tremble from the west.

They are going to return from the West, and, since Israel's lands bordered the Mediterranean Sea wherever they are, west would have to be west of the Holy Land itself!

> Hos 7:8 Ephraim, he hath mixed himself among the people; Ephraim is a cake not turned.

That is one of my favorite verses. The tribe of Ephraim is not only mixed among the nations, but it is also a bread not turned. What can that possibly mean? Well, the ancient Israelites baked their bread one side at a time, something like the pancakes we make today. It took time to bake one side, and more time to bake the other. At the time of Hosea, the Lord tells us that only one side of the bread is baked, in other words, Ephraim's history is only half over. For Ephraim's future, the cake would need to be turned and baked on the other side. God is telling us that half of Ephraim's saga was still future to this prophecy and that it would take place after their dispersion. So where did God put them?

> Hos 9:13-17 (*excerpts*) Ephraim ... is planted in a pleasant place: but Ephraim shall bring forth his children to the murderer ...[1] Oh Lord: what wilt thou give? give them a miscarrying womb and dry breasts...yea, though they bring forth, yet will I slay even the beloved fruit of their womb . . and they shall be wanderers among the nations.

---

[1] "Murderer" in Hebrew is: H2026. harag, haw-rag'; a prim. root; to smite with deadly intent: put to [death], make [slaughter], slay (-er), "Shall bring fourth his children to the murderer (slaughter)" In OT times, Israel "went forth to war." This is probably a figurative reference to warfare, to abortion, or to both.

Ephraim will be placed in a pleasant land, but in these terrible texts, we see that Ephraim's future would not always be pleasant. A warrior tribe still, they would be involved in foreign wars. And many of their children would die unborn, either through miscarriages or abortions. So who and where are they?

REVELATION'S "TIMES" IDENTIFIES EPHRAIM

The "time, times, and half a time" in Daniel were provably 2500 years, so unless there is a good scriptural reason to disregard that principle, Revelation's "times" should also be 2500 years.

> Rev 12:14 And to the woman [*Israel*] were given two wings of a great eagle, that she might fly into the wilderness, into her place, where she is nourished for **a time, and times, and half a time**, from the face of the serpent.

This 2500 year period cannot be in our future because there can be only *one* generation (forty years or so) following the time of the Gentiles and the time of the Gentiles is over (Luk 21:24-32). So to find out when this "time" fits, we need to lay this 2500 years over past history.

The last we heard of Israel was when they were taken captive into Assyria. Samaria, the capital of Israel, fell in 722BC. But the major captivity took place about two years earlier, circa 724BC. Hosea stated, "Ephraim is mixed with the nations," and his book was written just before the fall of Samaria. Could 724BC be when Revelation's "time, times, and half a time" began?[1] If so, then this *time* should lead us to a significant year in the history of Ephraim:

2500 - 724BC = 1776AD...The United States became a nation!

---

[1] The language of the verse does not tie us to the date of the destruction of Samaria. "Fly into the wilderness" speaks of the dispersion itself, and would be applicable for any time between 725-722BC.

GRAPH NUMBERS 14

3rd Time, Times & Half a Time

Deu 4:27 And the LORD shall scatter you among the nations, and ye shall be left few in number among the heathen, whither the LORD shall lead you.

Hos 2:15-16 And I will give her vineyards from thence, and the valley of Achor for a door of hope: and she shall sing there, as in the days of her youth, and as in the day when she came up out of the land of Egypt. And it shall be at that day, saith the LORD, that thou shalt call me Ishi; and shalt call me no more Baali.

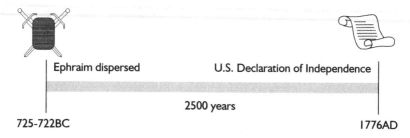

Ephraim dispersed   U.S. Declaration of Independence

2500 years

725-722BC   1776AD

Note: *Ishi* is Hebrew for husband, *Baali* is Hebrew for master. In the New Testament, the Church has a bride-bridegroom relationship with the Lord.

Is America the pleasant land where Ephraim was planted, and could the people who come from all over the world to seek freedom from tyranny and religious persecution be the descendants of those missing tribes? It certainly appears to be a possibility. For years people have been looking for the United States in prophecy. Now that we have found some evidence that this nation might contain the remnants of Ephraim and the ten lost tribes of Israel, do you suppose anyone will want to believe it? Not a chance. We would rather hang in there with the Seven-Year Tribulation view for which there is *NO* biblical or historic evidence whatsoever. But, unless we can think of some other incident of major prophetic importance that took place on or about 1776, then the United States becoming a nation is probably what that prophecy is about. That makes North America and the United States the pleasant and protected land where the Lord hid Ephraim (Hos 9:13).

THE DISPERSION

How most of the children of the ten dispersed tribes migrated to Europe is a story recorded by others.[1] Suffice to say that the heraldic symbols used by the great houses of Europe have their roots in the titles Jacob gave his twelve sons. If you question that, ask any authority on heraldry.[2] The coats of arms that people so proudly hang on their walls are straight out of Gen 49:1-27.

Throughout the Christian Era, the true saints of God were hounded all over Europe. The chronicles of the oppression of the true Church during the middle ages have to be read to be believed. Fox's *Book of Martyrs*, Thielman van Braght's *Martyr's Mirror* (the Anabaptist record), and Broadbent's *The Pilgrim Church* record the sufferings of our forefathers in detail. The true Christians had no settled home in any land, and their very lives were continually at risk. They wandered from place to place or were in hiding from persecution. They had a symbolic valley of Achor *(Achor means trouble)* throughout the middle ages. But the Lord told us it would be like that:

---

[1] To avoid any suggestion that the author is using material which is conjectural or lacks red-letter accreditation, only common historic knowledge and the Bible itself were used to support the conclusions in this chapter. However, for those interested in pursuing this line of study, here are a few books on the subject: *One Man's Destiny*, C.R. Dickey (Merrimac MA, Destiny Publishing); *Missing Links Discovered in Assyrian Tablets*, E. Raymond Capt (Thousand Oaks, CA, Artisan Sales); *The Royal House of Britain and Enduring Dynasties*, W. H. M. Milner (Windsor, Ontario, Canadian-British Israelite Association.)

[2] Heraldry is the profession, study, or art of devising, granting, and blazoning coats of arms, tracing genealogies, and determining and ruling on questions of rank or protocol, as exercised by an officer of arms.

> Heb 13:13-14 Let us go forth therefore unto him without the
> camp, bearing his reproach. For here have we no continuing
> city, but we seek one to come.

Then they cried unto the Lord and the Lord hid them from
their persecutors and planted them in a very pleasant land. It was
rich and fruitful and flowing with milk and honey. The New World
was just such a land, and the United States was founded by Christians fleeing religious persecution. God also told us exactly how
that was going to happen:

> Rev 12:15-17 And the serpent cast out of his mouth water as
> a flood after the woman, that he might cause her to be
> carried away of the flood. And the earth helped the woman,
> and the earth opened her mouth, and swallowed up the flood
> which the dragon cast out of his mouth. And the dragon was
> wroth with the woman, and went to make war with the rem-
> nant of her seed, which keep the commandments of God, and
> have the testimony of Jesus Christ.

In the verses above we read that Satan would try to destroy the
Jews and the Church with a flood of people.[1] But the Lord
separated a remnant church and many Jews from their enemies by
the Atlantic Ocean. This country grew and prospered and became
the hub of the Western world. West, West, where have I heard that
before? This hemisphere is as far West as you can get. Go any
farther and it is called the Far East.

> Hos 11:10-11 (*excerpts*) They shall walk after the LORD ...
> then the children shall tremble from the west ... and I will
> place them in their houses, saith the LORD.

Furthermore, the Church, like the Levites, is called to be priests
and to come out from the world.[2] God called Levi to be directly in

---

[1] "Waters" is figurative language for many peoples: Rev 17:15 "And he saith unto
me, The waters which thou sawest, where the whore sitteth, are peoples, and
multitudes, and nations, and tongues."

[2] 2Co 6:14-18, 1Pe 2:5-9, Rev 1:6, 5:10, and Rev 18:4-5.

the Lord's service. As priests, they were separated from the rest of the people. God even gave them special cities to live in:

Num 35:7 ... cities which ye shall give to the Levites shall be forty and eight cities: them shall ye give with their suburbs.

The Levites had 48 cities; the Continental United States has 48 states. It was not until after the pivotal year of 1948 that we too "mixed ourselves with the nations," (Hos 7:8) and states outside our borders were added. It was not until after 1948 that the United States began to lose its influence as the Christian lighthouse of the world. Occasional coincidences happen. But are all these historic fits just random chances that by some fluke of mathematical magic just happen to fit Scripture? That would be difficult for any thinking person to swallow. Here are another couple of "coincidences" of interest.

1. The Lord gave Abraham the covenant of circumcision. Until the last decade, babies were routinely circumcised in the United States. Why us? There is no sound medical reason for this practice.

2. The United States was the first nation to have a five-day work week, thus observing the Sabbath as well as Sunday.

3. Though Jacob had only 12 sons, Joseph's two sons became two tribes. Counting Ephraim and Manasseh, there were then actually thirteen tribes. In America there were only 12 colonies, but the Carolinas were too large to govern in horse and buggy days, so the Carolinas were split into two states, North and South Carolina. So as Israel's twelve sons became thirteen tribes, our twelve colonies became thirteen states.

All that was long ago. Since then the United States has fought a half-dozen foreign wars: bringing her "children forth to the murderer," as foretold in Hosea 9:13. And now, through manifold abortions, we also bring our children forth to the murderer in a new and savage way. However, terrible as that may sound, God's eternal plan is still on schedule.

EZEKIEL'S TWO STICKS

Just before Ezekiel describes the battle of Armageddon in the 38th and 39th chapters of his book, he tells of the restoration of the Jews to the Holy Land in the vision of the "dry bones." Noting the context, these dry-bones were fulfilled in Israel in 1948.

> Eze 37:11-12 Son of man, these bones are the whole house of Israel: behold, they say, Our bones are dried, and our hope is lost: we are cut off for our parts ... Therefore prophesy and say unto them, Thus saith the Lord GOD; Behold, O my people, I will **open your graves,** and cause you to come up out of your graves, and bring you into the land of Israel.

Armageddon follows closely at the heels of this prophecy. How soon will that battle be? End-time pundits notwithstanding, Scripture doesn't seem to say. However, because of where we are in history, we can now cross-reference those dry-bones with one of Daniel's final prophecies and get a time pin:

> Dan 12:1-2 And at that time shall Michael stand up, the great prince which standeth for the children of thy people: and there shall be a time of trouble, such as never was since there was a nation even to that same time: and at that time thy people shall be delivered, every one that shall be found written in the book. And many of them that sleep in the **dust of the earth** shall awake, some to everlasting life, and some to shame and ever-lasting contempt.

As the Lord put flesh on the dry-bones lying in their graves (Eze 37:11), so those who slept in the dust awoke, to be restored to the Holy Land (Dan 12:1-2). Same event, different figurative language. As an interesting side note, God tells us that all who came to life (returned to Israel) would not be believers. However, despite their spiritual condition, the Lord is assembling the forces that are going to take a stand for Him in the final battle:

> Eze 37:16 Moreover, thou son of man, take thee one stick, and write upon it, For Judah, and for the children of Israel his companions: then take another stick, and write upon it, For

Joseph, the stick of Ephraim and for all the house of Israel his companions:

All agree that the above is an end-time vision. Simply stated, Ephraim and the ten northern tribes are one stick, while Judah (the Jews) is the other. As we look about us now, something wonderful is happening to both the Jews and the ten lost tribes, something we have been waiting to see for 2700 years:

Isa 11:13 The envy also of Ephraim shall depart, and the adversaries of Judah shall be cut off: Ephraim shall not envy Judah, and Judah shall not vex Ephraim.

Before the end, the Lord will take the stick of Ephraim, now in the true Church, and unite it with the stick of Judah, and we will be one stick in God's hand.

Eze 37:19 Say unto them, Thus saith the Lord GOD; Behold, I will take the stick of Joseph, which is in the hand of Ephraim, and the tribes of Israel his fellows, and will put them with him, even with the stick of Judah, and make them one stick, and they shall be one in mine hand.

It appears that God plans to make one stick (one people) of Israel and Judah again. He is going to heal the division between them and draw them together. Within this generation, the Christians will be united with the Jewish people, and we will be one people again. The Israel of God. Are we up to the task ahead? Of course not, but now that our hearts can be opened to who Ephraim and Judah are, we can just begin to see what our end-time roles will be:

Zec 9:13 When I have bent Judah for me, filled the bow with Ephraim, and raised up thy sons, O Zion, against thy sons, O Greece, and made thee as the sword of a mighty man.

Judah, now back in the Holy Land, will have only one true ally: Ephraim and the Gentile church. We are the only candidate left in the world for the title of "the stick of Joseph." The days when the United States was a trustworthy ally to Israel are swiftly passing, as our governmental leaders bend to the wishes of the Palestinian Moslems and dip Old Glory into the inescapable tar-pit of Islamic oil.

There is only a remnant of the true Church left in any western land now. As Scripture opens before us, we can see that the remnant may be from the lost tribes of Israel, whom Satan has always hated (Rev 12:17). Don't be lulled to sleep, folks. If the Lord doesn't provide a way of escape, physical persecution is close at hand for Christians everywhere:

> Rev 12:11-12 And they overcame him by the blood of the Lamb, and by the word of their testimony; and they loved not their lives unto the death. Therefore rejoice, *ye* heavens, and ye that dwell in them. Woe to the inhabiters of the earth and of the sea! for the devil is come down unto you, having great wrath, because he knoweth that he hath but a short time.

So, were 1948 and 1967 important dates? In those years, the new nation of Israel was born and the time of the Two Witnesses came to an end. Jerusalem was freed, and all day=years and time-times were fulfilled. We are now in the end-times, the final generation, and God is assembling His forces for the hour of trial (Rev 3:10) and the battle of Armageddon. The true Church is part of those forces, and the other part is ...

Timeless Covenant

CHAPTER 10

Do not abhor us, for thy name's sake,
do not disgrace the throne of thy glory:
remember, break not thy covenant with us.

JER 14:21

MANY wonder how a lost Jewish people could possibly be one of the Two Witnesses, quoting as support for their view, "There is no other name under heaven, given among men, whereby ye must be saved" (Act 4:12). Their concern is reasonable enough. So how can the true Church be the ally of a people who don't know that Jesus is their Messiah? Well, when we look back at the rest of the Bible in the light of what we now know from Revelation, we get a clearer picture of the spiritual position of the Jews during this era. But to see it, we also need to understand the spiritual condition of the Old Testament saints. Were the Old Testament Israelites "born again" like New Testament Christians are? There are a few heavyweight theologians who would dispute the point, so let's bring Scripture to bear on the issue.[1]

In His discussion with Nicodemus (John 3), Jesus put a name to what happens in the human heart when we first turn to the Lord. He called it being "born again." When Jesus spoke with Nicodemus, the cross was still in Jesus' future, yet right there He made a doctrinal statement that many think applies only to the Church:

---

[1] Joh 3:3, 3:7 and 1Pe 1:23 are the only verses in the Bible where this experience is so named.

> Joh 3:3,10 Jesus answered and said unto him, Verily, verily,
> I say unto thee, Except a man be born again, he cannot see
> the kingdom of God ... Art thou a master of Israel, and
> knowest not these things?

Even though the Old Testament was all the Scripture Nicodemus had, the Lord expected him to understand what being born
again was all about. So here is the question: How could Nicodemus
have understood the born-again principle before Jesus died on the
cross? Answer: He could only have understood being born again
before the cross if Old Testament believers *could* be born again
before the cross. Jesus expected Nicodemus to know, as did a
scribe of his time, that it was not correct doctrine, but a changed
heart that resulted in salvation:

> Mar 12:32-33 And the scribe said unto him, Well, Master,
> thou hast said the truth: for there is one God; and there is
> none other but he: And to love him with all the heart, and
> with all the understanding, and with all the soul, and with all
> the strength, to love his neighbour as himself, is more than all
> whole burnt offerings and sacrifices.

The Old Testament is full of verses declaring that a changed
heart, rather than sacrifice, is the central aspect of salvation.[1] The
whole 11th chapter of Hebrews teaches that Old Testament saints
were saved by faith. They were not justified by the Levitical code,
nor by the deeds of the law any more than we are. Old Testament
believers were given a changed heart before the cross – were born
again – just like Christians are after the cross.

---

[1] Here are four of many Old Testament verses that stress heart condition unto
salvation above ritualistic observance:
Gen 15:6 And he believed in the LORD; and he counted it to him for righteousness.
Hab 2:4 Behold, his soul which is lifted up is not upright in him: but the just shall
live by his faith.
Psa 51:16-17 For thou desirest not sacrifice; else would I give it: thou delightest
not in burnt offering. The sacrifices of God are a broken spirit: a broken and a
contrite heart, O God, thou wilt not despise.
Mic 6:8 ... what doth the LORD require of thee, but to do justly, and to love mercy,
and to walk humbly with thy God?

Since Jesus said, "Except a man be born again he cannot see the kingdom of heaven," then Noah, Abraham, Moses, David, Elijah, Job, Daniel, and all the rest of the Old Testament saints had to be born again, or we will not see them in Heaven. We saw Moses and Elijah in their glorified bodies on the Mount of Transfiguration – before the cross – so we can prove they were born again, unless we wish to believe that God would permit His glory to radiate through the faces of the unregenerate. Obviously, those elder brethren had changed hearts, and a changed heart is what being born again is all about.

Eze 36:26-27 A new heart also will I give you, and a new spirit will I put within you: and I will take away the stony heart out of your flesh, and I will give you an heart of flesh.And I will put my spirit within you, and cause you to walk in my statutes, and ye shall keep my judgments, and do them.

Old Testament or New, there is NO difference in how a soul is saved. The only difference is doctrine, and doctrine is determined by how the Lord willed to reveal Himself to man at a given time. Old Testament saints and Christians have different doctrines, but the method of salvation is the same.

1Co 10:1-4 I would not that ye should be ignorant, how that all our fathers were under the cloud, and all passed through the sea. And were all baptized unto Moses in the cloud and in the sea; And did all eat the same spiritual meat; And did all drink the same spiritual drink: for they drank of that spiritual Rock that followed them: and that Rock was Christ.

True saints have always been born again "by grace through faith," regardless of the era in which they lived. This is a major issue in some churches, so please make an effort to understand the argument. It will be important to your spiritual well-being and will aid you in your future comprehension of the Bible.

We said all that to get to this: When Jesus went to the cross, there were Old Testament Jews, spread all over the world. They were in Africa, Spain, India, even as far away as England. If they were true believers, they were born again. Elect, just like you and I are (Rom 11:28). Many of them must have been unaware of Jesus' ministry, death, and resurrection.

So here's the question: Did those dispersed Jews lose their salvation the moment Jesus went to the cross and they were suddenly and unknowingly thrust into the Christian Era? If we believe so, then we are saying a man is saved by his doctrine, rather than his heart condition.

If a Jew, under God's covenants given to him through the patriarchs and prophets, could be saved by faith in his coming Messiah for one nanosecond into the Christian Era, then a Jew *in that same spiritual condition* can be saved under those same covenants a thousand, or even 2000 years later. The only way that would not be true is if salvation is based upon where we are positioned in history, and the correctness of our doctrine.

Numerous times in the Old Testament the Lord speaks of His everlasting covenant with the children of Israel, including the following verses:

> Gen 7:7 And I will establish my covenant between me and thee and thy seed after thee in their generations for an everlasting covenant, to be a God unto thee, and to thy seed after thee.

> Psa 105:8-10 He hath remembered his covenant for ever, the word which he commanded to a thousand generations ... And confirmed the same unto Jacob for a law, and to Israel for an everlasting covenant.

If faith in God's Old Testament covenant was good enough to save Moses and Elijah, then it is good enough to save a Jew today *if* – and it is a big *if* – the Holy Spirit has not revealed to that Jew that Yeshua is his Messiah. When the Holy Spirit does so, the Jew needs to recognize God's Son as his Messiah and Lord just like we do. So is it possible for a Jew in this information age to be unaware that Yeshua[1] is his Messiah?[2] Jesus gave us a marvelous parable in Luke which explains it very clearly:

> Luk 5:33-39 (*excerpts*) And they [*the scribes and Pharisees*] said unto him, Why do the disciples of John fast often, and make prayers, and likewise the disciples of the Pharisees; but thine eat and drink? And he said unto them, Can ye make the children of the bridechamber fast, while the bridegroom is with them?... And he spake also a parable unto them; No man putteth a piece of a new garment upon an old; if otherwise, then both the new maketh a rent, and the piece that was taken out of the new agreeth not with the old. And no man putteth new wine into old bottles; else the new wine will burst the bottles, and be spilled, and the bottles shall perish. But new wine must be put into new bottles; and both are preserved.

The Pharisees were questioning why Jesus' disciples didn't keep Jewish traditions. Jesus replied that the children of the bridegroom didn't fast while the bridegroom was present, speaking of Himself and the disciples. He then likened the gospel to new wine, and the Jews to old wineskins. Jesus went on to say that He would not put the new wine of the gospel into the old wineskins of the Jewish people, lest He destroy them both. Jesus concluded with the categorical statement that He did not will for the old bottles to perish, so new wine was put in new wineskins, *and both would be preserved.* That is a mystery indeed. How can a Jew be

---

[1] Strong's No. H3091. Yehowshuwa', yeh-ho-shoo'-ah; or Yehowshu'a, yeh-ho-shoo'-ah; from H3068 and H3467; Jehovah-saved; Jehoshua (i.e. Joshua), the Jewish leader: Jehoshua, Jehoshuah, Joshua. Compare H1954, H3442. Transliterated into Greek as Jesus, many Jews spell His name in the abbreviated form of Y'shua, Yeshua or Yeshuah.

[2] It is no easier to tell if a Jew is saved than it is to tell the spiritual condition of a Gentile. But, if the Holy Spirit reveals to a Jew that Jesus is his Messiah, he is no longer blind. If a Jew then rejects the Lord, he is as lost as any Gentile who does. Consequently, a witness to Jews is as necessary as it is for Gentiles. If a Jew already has the circumcision of the heart (Rom 2:28-29), and the Holy Spirit takes the veil away, the believing Jew WILL turn to Yeshua. Why? Because, the same Spirit that takes the veil away will point him straight to God's Son. Only the Lord knows the true heart condition, (1Sa 16:7).

preserved if he does not understand the gospel? Let's see how God accomplished it. He promised Moses He would:

> Lev 26:33-45 (*excerpts*) I will scatter you among the heathen, and will draw out a sword after you ... And they that are left of you shall pine away in their iniquity in your enemies' lands ... And yet for all that, when they be in the land of their enemies, I will not cast them away, neither will I abhor them, to destroy them utterly, and to break my covenant with them: for I am the LORD their God . . But I will for their sakes remember the covenant of their ancestors, whom I brought forth out of the land of Egypt in the sight of the heathen, that I might be their God: I am the LORD.

ELECTION FOR BOTH COVENANTS

Throughout the centuries, the Holy Spirit has kept the Jew under the law (2Co 3:14, Gal 5:2-3). As stated before, to the Jew, the Old Testament is all the Bible there is. To him, Messiah is still to come, and oh, how he longs for His appearance, just as we do. The Jew believes in Him and trusts in Him because of the promises of God given to him in the Old Testament. Can his faith be in vain? The Bible tells us, if we only have ears to hear it:

> Rom 11:8-11 (According as it is written, God hath given them the spirit of slumber, eyes that they should not see, and ears that they should not hear) unto this day. I say then, Have they stumbled that they should fall? God forbid: but *rather* through their fall salvation *is come* unto the Gentiles, for to provoke them to jealousy.[1]

> Rom 11:24-25 For if thou [*the Gentile church*] wert cut out of the olive tree which is wild by nature, and wert grafted contrary to nature into a good olive tree [*the Jews*]: how

[1] Some have suggested that it is impossible for a Jew in this age not to know about Jesus. If we were dealing in the natural realm, the author would agree, but we are not. By a sovereign act of divine will, God blinded the spiritual eyes of the Jews (Rom 11:8) and only God can cause them to see again! If the Lord blinded the Jews to their eternal damnation, then He broke faith with the Patriarchs, and His everlasting covenants with Israel are untrue. Num 23:19 states, "God is not a man, that he should lie; neither the son of man, that he should repent: hath he said, and shall he not do it? or hath he spoken, and shall he not make it good?"

much more shall these, which be the natural *branches,* be grafted into their own olive tree? For I would not, brethren, that ye [*Gentiles*] should be ignorant of this mystery, lest ye should be wise in your own conceits; that blindness in part is happened to Israel, until the fulness of the Gentiles be come in.

Rom 11:28-29 As concerning the gospel, *they* [*the Jews*] *are* enemies for your sakes: but as touching the election,[1] *they* [*the Jews*] *are* beloved for the fathers' sakes. For the gifts and calling of God *are* without repentance. [*are irrevocable, NASB*]

Note the two groups of people in those verses: *We* and *They.* Language is meant to communicate, and in no language known to man are *we* and *they* the same group of people. These are two distinctly different bodies of people. From context, these two groups are the Jewish people and the Gentile church. According to Rom 11:28, one of these two groups is the enemy of the Gospel. The Church is not the enemy of the Gospel, so the other group must be, and that's the Jewish people.

But despite their enmity to the truth of the gospel, wonder of wonders, they are still elect. Hear that: the Jews are still elect. That is not a suppositional doctrine; Rom 11:28-29 states they are still elect, and the following verses affirm it:

Rom 11:30-32 For as ye [*the Gentiles*] in times past have not believed God, yet have now obtained mercy through their [*the Jews*] unbelief: Even so have these [*Jews*] also now not believed, that through your mercy [*shown to the Gentiles*] they [*the Jews*] also may obtain mercy. For God hath concluded them all [*both Jews and Gentiles*] in unbelief, that he might have mercy upon all.

Those Scriptures lead us to this point: If the Church is "elect," and Israel is "elect," wherein lies the difference between us? Only in our historic position, and in the accuracy of our doctrine *(neither of which saves us).* The Old Testament saints knew their Messiah

---

[1] Strong's No. 1589. ekloge, ek-log-ay'; from G1586; (divine) selection: chosen, election.

was coming, even though they did not know who He was going to be. They were born again, even though they did not know His identity. They were saved by faith in the same Messiah that you and I are, and not by their doctrine. Praise God we are not saved because our doctrines are perfect, but because Jesus is the perfect atonement for our sins, and His blood is perfect even for the Jews who do not know His name.

Over the last 22 years, I have watched people dance all around Rom 11:11 and 11:24-32. I even know several theological types who heatedly declare, "I don't know what those verses mean, but they certainly don't mean what they say," thus putting the doctrines of men above the Word of God. Why not believe what those verses say? Is the Bible the Word of God, or isn't it? I fear our traditions are so firmly entrenched that only a major disaster or the return of the Lord will change them. Throughout the Christian Era, we have been trying to make Gentiles out of Jews, but we have it backwards. Israel was not grafted into the Church; the Church was grafted into Israel (Rom 11:17).

In Rom 11:25, we were commanded not to become "wise in our own conceits" because we were given the gospel while the Jews were not. But we got arrogant anyway, and it has resulted in our own blindness. We've been thinking all along that we had it all, while the Jews were without hope. It isn't so, but unless we permit the Holy Spirit to take the scales from our eyes, we will remain hopelessly blinded to God's overall plan.

BREAD AND WINE

Jesus was surrounded by a jeering crowd as He stood before Pilate. Pilate wanted to free Him, but the crowd demanded His crucifixion. The Lord loved them, taught them, fed them and healed everyone who came to Him. The Pharisees knew who He was, but they still wanted Him dead:

Mat 27:22-25 Pilate saith unto them, What shall I do then with Jesus which is called Christ? *They* all say unto him, Let him be crucified. And the governor said, Why, what evil hath he done? But they cried out the more, saying, Let him be crucified. When Pilate saw that he could prevail nothing, but *that* rather a tumult was made, he took water, and washed *his* hands before the multitude, saying, I am innocent of the blood of this just person: see ye *to it.* Then answered all the people, and said, **His blood** *be* **on us, and on our children.**

How are we saved, brethren? Because Jesus' blood is upon us. There at the Pavement, the Jews uttered what they thought to be a curse, "His blood be on us, and on our children." But I don't believe God saw it that way. With unfathomable love and mercy He looked down on the people He had blinded for our sakes and probably said, "Be it unto you in accordance with your words."

Despite the Jews not recognizing God's dying Son as their Messiah, the Lord put His merciful hand over the eyes of His beloved people Israel, and saved them. Do we even begin to grasp the caring and forgiving nature of our Heavenly Father? All He needed to do for them to be lost was nothing, just nothing. Instead of that, He blinded them so they could not sin against a knowledge of the truth.[1] Oh, what it has cost those precious people. What sufferings they have endured throughout the centuries because of their inability to see the Savior who went to the cross for them.[2] Spiritually, they suffer still, looking dimly ahead, through darkened Old Testament eyes, for the coming of their beloved Messiah.

---

[1] Heb 10:26 For if we sin wilfully after that we have received the knowledge of the truth [*that Jesus is the only sacrifice for sin that is acceptable to God the Father*], there remaineth no more sacrifice for sins, But a certain fearful looking for of judgment and fiery indignation, which shall devour the adversaries.

[2] Certainly many of the Pharisees rejected the Lord so as to be lost, but not all. Nicodemus and Joseph of Arimathea are notable exceptions. Nor would it surprise the author to see Gamaliel in Heaven. He defended the brethren in Acts 5:37-39, and that he feared the Lord is unquestionable.

108 *The False Prophet*

> Rom 11:33-36 O the depth of the riches both of the wisdom and knowledge of God! how unsearchable are his judgments, and his ways past finding out! For who hath known the mind of the Lord? or who hath been his counsellor? Or who hath first given to him, and it shall be recompensed unto him again? For of him, and through him, and to him, are all things: to whom be glory for ever. Amen.

Looking at the big picture, why did the Lord decree a partial spiritual blindness upon His beloved people? It was for the sake of you and me, the Gentile believers. How dare the Church judge a people whom God Himself has blinded. The Lord desires that we have a loving and understanding heart toward our brethren afar-off, the people who were "blinded for our sake," moving them to jealousy so that they come to His Son.

Most Jews believe that Christians hate them. They may not show it up front, but down inside the Jews believe it, and for a very good reason. It is a deplorable fact that many so-called Christians have persecuted the Jews throughout this era in the mistaken belief that they killed Jesus. My, have our spiritual eyes ever been dulled. It wasn't the Jews who killed Jesus. You and I killed Jesus! Don't you see that Jesus sacrificed Himself because you and I sinned? While Jesus was hanging on the cross, He saw the sins of all time, from the first sin of Adam until the very last sin to be committed. It was for your sins and mine that He said, "Father forgive them, for they know not what they do."

Blindness is upon Israel until the fullness of the Gentiles is come in (Rom 11:25). Maybe that day is at hand now because many thousands of Jews are now turning to Yeshua. But the Lord has yet to take the scales from the eyes of all, and many Jews still look to Moses and the prophets.

In Hebrews we read about Father Abraham giving tithes to Melchizedek (the Lord Jesus). Abraham did so for all those who would proceed from his loins: for his children throughout all generations to come (Heb 7:1-10). Now what was Melchizedek's response to Abraham? He set a table before him, and on that table, bread and wine (Gen 14:17-20). Bread and wine ... the same communion that Jesus served the disciples at the last supper. Oh, the richness of the foreknowledge of God. Do we have eyes to see what the Lord Jesus did through Abraham, and for his physical seed forever? As Abraham gave tithes for the children of Israel yet to be born, so, in like manner, Jesus had communion with all the children of Israel yet to be born, and our God is a covenant-keeping God.[1]

> Jer 31:3-8 Yea, I have loved thee with an everlasting love: therefore with lovingkindness have I drawn thee. For there shall be a day, *that* the watchmen upon the mount Ephraim shall cry, Arise ye, and let us go up to Zion unto the LORD our God. For thus saith the LORD; Sing with gladness for Jacob, and shout among the chief of the nations: publish ye, praise ye, and say, O LORD, save thy people, the remnant of Israel.

If the Jewish people had come to know Jesus as their Messiah, they would have been absorbed into the Church, and Jews would have disappeared from the face of the earth. That doesn't sound so bad, does it? How significant could that be?

If the Jewish people had accepted Yeshua as their Messiah, then the Jewish nation, as a distinct people, would have been absorbed into the Church and the prophecies we have been studying could never have been fulfilled!

The fulfillment of every prophecy we have looked at so far, plus the ones we study next, depended on the Jews not knowing Jesus as their Messiah!

---

[1] Most denominations believe that the Jews of the Christian Era who are blind to the fact that Jesus is their Savior are lost. Nonetheless, the scriptural evidence to the contrary is so strong that the author wonders how the Church has been able to maintain their position.

Leopard-Bear-Lion

CHAPTER 11

I will bring the worst of the heathen,

and they shall possess their houses:

I will also make the pomp of the strong to cease;

and their holy places shall be defiled.

EZE 7:24

JUST about now you are probably saying, "So that's who the Lord's forces are, but what about this antichrist? Aren't the beasts of Revelation about him and his army, and isn't he supposed to give the unsaved a mark in their hands or on their foreheads?

Well, now that we understand day=years, it's obvious that at least part of Revelation is less about the end-times than it is about the Holy Land during the Christian Era. Is it possible that the rest of Revelation is also being fulfilled in the Holy Land during this era? Lets look at that possibility.

The following verse was written on mount Nebo in 1406BC. Moses was about to die and this declaration is in his final oration to the Children of Israel just before they enter the land of Canaan.

> Deu 11:11-12 But the land, whither ye go to possess it, *is* a land of hills and valleys, *and* drinketh water of the rain of heaven: A land which the LORD thy God careth for: the eyes of the LORD thy God *are* always upon it, from the beginning of the year even unto the end of the year.

The Lord's eyes are still upon the Holy Land. Do you think the Lord has forgotten His promises about the land where Abraham offered up Isaac, where His temple was built, "a house of prayer for all people"? The land where His Son died, "not only for our sins, but for the sins of the whole world"? (1Jo 2:2)[1]. Of course not, and that land is not holy to the Jews alone. We have been adopted into Israel (Gal 3:29). If the land of Canaan is holy to the Jews, it is holy to us. If Jerusalem is a Holy City to the Jews, then it is a Holy City to the Church.[2]

> Gal 6:15-16 For in Christ Jesus neither circumcision availeth any thing, nor uncircumcision, but a new creature. And as many as walk according to this rule, peace *be* on them, and mercy, and upon the Israel of God.

TIMES AND FOUR EMPIRES

All of Revelation's day=years and "times" were fulfilled by 1967, *in the Holy Land,* so we should look at the possibility that other prophecies in Revelation, like its three Beasts, might also be fulfilled there.

Knowledge is cumulative. We had to understand that prophetic days were really years before we could identify the Dome of the Rock as the Abomination of Desolation. Only then could we understand the significance of the Moslems in Bible prophecy. We also had to understand day=years to identify the Two Witnesses. Only then could we understand the spiritual position of Jews during this era. In the same way, we now need to know about the four beasts of Daniel 7 before we can identify the Leopard-Bear-Lion Beast of Revelation 13.

Keep in mind that Revelation is a figurative book. It is full of concepts expressed in a pictorial way such as *beasts, horns, seals,*

---

[1] If you question that concept, please read 2Ch 7:12-16 and Eze 43:7. These verses are not alone; Gen 16:18-21, 17:8, Num 34:1-15, Jos 21:43, Exo 23:31 and Act 7:5 also affirm that the land of Canaan is eternally Holy unto the Lord.

[2] In Daniel and Revelation, God reveals the future of the Holy Land and the future of His people, the "Israel of God," both Jew and Gentile. Daniel was positioned at the beginning of Gentile domination of the Holy Land, 606BC, so he is a prophet to "the time of the Gentiles." With the exception of those few verses which relate to the ultimate time of the end (Dan 8:19-25), Daniel's book was fulfilled in 1967AD. John, on the other hand, was positioned in 95AD, at the beginning of the Christian Era, so he is obviously the prophet to the Christian Era.

trumpets, candlesticks and *bowls.* If we are to understand God's intent for these figures, we need to find out what they mean. Let's first look at a couple within the Bowls of Wrath:

> Rev 16:1-2 (NASB) And I heard a loud voice from the temple, saying to the seven angels, "Go and pour out the seven bowls of the wrath of God into the earth." And the first *angel* went and poured out his bowl into the earth; and it became a loathsome and malignant sore upon the men who had the mark of the beast and who worshiped his image.

Not for a minute does anyone believe that there will be holy angels up in Heaven pouring out an alphabet soup of trials on Earth from huge gold-rimmed alabaster "bowls." Many severe trials are indeed going to come upon the Earth, but enormous bowls full? Not very likely. It is more reasonable to conclude that God is using "bowl" figuratively, to show us the vast quantity and severity of the trials coming upon the earth.

Nor does anyone believe that we are going to have a flaming red, ten-horned, seven-headed dinosaur roaring about the land, with an all-decked-out, blood-drinking "lady of the night" riding on its back (the Scarlet Beast of Rev 17:3). Nor are we likely to see a real, living animal that is a cross between a leopard, bear and lion all rolled up into one, with blasphemous names tattooed all over its seven heads (the composite beast of Rev 13:2). Nor are we likely to hear a spirited oration from a stone idol that looks like that beast (the image of Rev 13:15). However, if we interpret Revelation literally, that is what we have to believe because that is what Revelation says. Since none of the above is even remotely sensible, then Revelation must be figurative in nature. God's eternal plan given to us in pictorial language.

Now, figurative language is as different from literal language as Japanese is from English. If Japanese were the only language I spoke and you wished to tell me something, you would need to speak to me in Japanese. If you addressed me in English, I wouldn't understand a word you said. Some of your words might sound familiar and I might even try to make sense of them, but I would only be guessing, and probably guessing wrong. Well, Revelation is written in a special language, too – a pictorial one. Revelation cannot be understood unless you "speak" the pictorial language in which it was written.

So let's look at the pictorial language God used to tell the Jews about the nations who were going to rule in the Holy Land during the "Time of the Gentiles." This is a rather lengthy quote and commentary, but I don't know of a better way to explain these verses. Comments are set within the Bible text itself, in *italics*. Please study the passage carefully because your ability to identify the beasts in Revelation will depend upon your understanding of these principles:[1]

> Dan 7:3-4 And four great beasts came up from the sea [*the sea is the peoples and nations of the world, Rev 17:15*], diverse one from another. The first *was* like a lion [*The national emblem of Babylon was the winged lion*], and had eagle's wings [*The Ishtar gate of that city has bass reliefs of winged lions upon it*]: I beheld till the wings thereof were plucked, and it was lifted up from the earth, and made stand upon the feet as a man [*The Neo-Babylonian Empire, begun under Nebopolasser, was brought to the peak of its power by his son Nebuchadnezzar, (606-562BC). Nebuchadnezzar was the most absolute monarch in all human history*], and a man's heart was given to it [*Also a reference to Nebuchadnezzar, who came to the Lord late in life, Dan 4:37*].
>
> Dan 7:5 And behold another beast, a second, like to a bear [*After Babylon was taken in 536BC, Medo-Persia became the dominant world power*], and it raised up itself on one side [*The Persians were "raised up" over and ruled the Medean half of their empire*], and *it had* three ribs in the mouth of it between the teeth of it [*The Medo-Persians conquered three*

---

[1] This prophecy was given to Daniel in 552BC. Daniel lived at the beginning of the time of the Gentiles, so his prophecies look forward at world history from the beginning of that time. The identity of these beasts has been understood by the church for centuries and this view is accepted by most conservative theologians.

other empires: Lydia, Babylon, and Egypt]: and they said thus unto it, Arise, devour much flesh.

Dan 7:6 After this I beheld, and lo another, like a leopard, which had upon the back of it four wings of a fowl [*Alexander the Great defeated the Medo-Persian Empire at the Battle of Issus, in 332BC*]; the beast had also four heads [*Alexander had four great generals under him*]; and dominion was given to it [*After Alexander died in Babylon, 323BC, his empire was divided between his four generals: Ptolemy, Selucius, Lycimicus, and Cassander*].

Dan 7:7 After this I saw in the night visions, and behold a fourth beast, dreadful and terrible, and strong exceedingly; and it had great iron teeth: it devoured and brake in pieces, and stamped the residue with the feet of it [*Rome destroyed the remnants of the divided Grecian Empire and began to control the Holy Land in 65BC – The Roman Empire continued until 476AD*]: and it *was* diverse from all the beasts that *were* before it; and it had ten horns [*After Rome fell, it was divided into roughly ten Eastern and western nations which have continued to this day.*].

Dan 7:8 I considered the horns, and, behold, there came up among them another little horn, before whom there were three of the first horns plucked up by the roots [*Adolf Hitler – The Nazi regime controlled most of the geographic area of the old Roman Empire. Which three nations the Lord is talking about here is open to question, however Nazi Germany did pull surrounding states up by the roots*]: and, behold, in this horn were eyes like the eyes of man [*Same expression as is used to describe Nebuchadnezzar, so the Lord is telling us of a single king with absolute power*], and a mouth speaking great things [*Dan 7:11 continues on to tell us of the fall of Nazi Germany, which was the death-knell of the Roman Empire*].

Dan 7:12 As concerning the rest of the beasts [*Lion-Bear-Leopard or Babylon, Medo-Persia and Greece*] they had their dominion taken away: yet their lives were prolonged for a season and time [*After Rome fell, the Holy Land again came under the dominion of the descendants of the three first beasts, Babylon, Medo-Persia, and Greece. They came back into power as the 1st Islamic Jihad of 634AD. They conquered Jerusalem in*

639AD, and ruled that city for most of the Christian Era. A time of 1000 years, plus a season of 250 years=1250 years. The Moslems ruled in the Holy Land for 1260 years, from 688 to 1948AD].

Dan 7:17-20 These great beasts, which are four, are four kings [*or kingdoms*], which shall arise out of the earth. But the saints of the most High [*the Jews were the saints during Daniel's time*] shall take the kingdom [*i.e., the Holy land*], and possess the kingdom for ever, even for ever and ever. Then I would know the truth of the fourth beast [*Rome*], which was diverse from all the others, exceeding dreadful, whose teeth *were of* iron, and his nails *of* brass; *which* devoured, brake in pieces, and stamped the residue with his feet [*Rome dominated the known world for over 400 years*]; And of the ten horns that *were* in his head [*the Roman Empire divided into many smaller states including the major European nations we know today*], and *of* the other which came up, and before whom three fell; even *of* that horn that had eyes, and a mouth that spake very great things [*Adolf Hitler*], whose look *was* more stout than his fellows [*The Hitler regime. Nazi Germany was the last gasp of the old militaristic Roman Empire*].

Dan 7:21-22 I beheld, and the same horn [*Hitler*] made war with the saints, and prevailed against them [*the Jews were the saints when God gave Daniel this prophecy, and 6,000,000 Jews were killed by the Nazis*]; Until the Ancient of days came, and judgment was given to the saints of the most High; and the time came that the saints possessed the kingdom [*and in 1948 the Jews did indeed become a nation again*].

Dan 7:23-24 Thus he said, The fourth beast shall be the fourth kingdom upon earth [*This is how we know that this passage is not about just individual kings, but really about kingdoms or empires*], which shall be diverse from all kingdoms, and shall devour the whole earth, and shall tread it down, and break it in pieces. And the ten horns out of this kingdom *are* ten kings *that* shall arise: and another shall rise after them; and he shall be diverse from the first, and he shall subdue three kings [*Austria, France and Italy were indeed subdued by Hitler during WW2*].[1]

Dan 7:25　And he shall speak *great* words against the most High [*Satan speaks out against the Most High, so now God is telling Daniel about the vast unseen spiritual battle taking place all around us*], and shall wear out the saints of the most High [*When this was written, in 552BC, the Jews were all the saints there were*], and think to change times and laws[2] [*Islam begins counting its years in 622AD and ignores the Sabbath*]: and they shall be given into his hand until a time and times and the dividing of time [*The Jews were given into the enemy's hand from 552BC, when this prophecy was given, until the new nation of Israel, 1948AD. That is 2½ x 1000 or 2500 years*].[3]

IDENTITY OF THE LEOPARD-BEAR-LION

Now the most important thing to notice in the above quote is that the "beasts" in Daniel were *not* conquerors or kings. In fact, they were not people at all. Those "beasts" were empires. Nowhere in the Bible has the Lord changed the definition for "beasts," and that key unlocks the hidden identity of the "beasts" in Revelation. It's a pretty obvious key once you see it:

*The Biblical definition for beasts
is kingdoms or empires!*

---

[1] Dan 7 is not an end-time prophecy. Dan 8:17-19 identifies the little-horn out of the He-Goat (Greece) as the final enemy of Israel and the Church. Since Syria-Lebanon was recognized as Grecian during John's time, the final enemy leader to come against Israel will be Moslem, probably out of the Syria-Lebanon area.

[2] June 25th, 622 AD marked the turning point in Islam as Muhammad migrated (Hijra) to Yatrib (now Medina) and was declared as head of state and commander in chief of the first Islamic Umma (community of believers). Moslems start their dating from that year. Thus, according to Islam, we are in the fifteenth century not the twentieth.

[3] Since it is evident that this "time, times and half a time" was fulfilled in 1948AD, regardless of who we wish to claim as the "Little Horn" of Dan 7, that person would have to be placed before 1948. Looking at history, it appears that Adolf Hitler and the German Third Reich accurately fulfill this 4th beast.

Daniel 7 firmly establishes the figurative identity of the first three Middle Eastern empires that dominated the Holy Land after the fall of the Kingdom of Judah:

Lion = BABYLON.
Bear = MEDO-PERSIA
Leopard = GREECE

The modern counterparts of those beasts are:

Lion = IRAQ
Bear = IRAN
Leopard = SYRIA-LEBANON

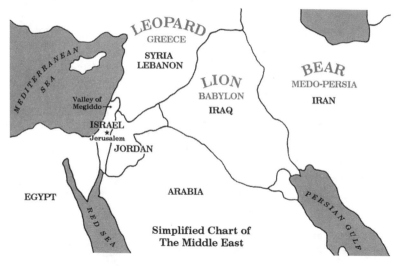

Simplified Chart of
The Middle East

Nowhere in the Bible have those figurative identities been changed. Throughout Scripture, Lion remains Babylon or Iraq, Bear remains Medo-Persia or Iran, and Leopard remains Greece or Syria-Lebanon. So when we read about a beast in Revelation with those same names, we have every reason to believe the Lord is telling us of the offspring of those empires:

> Rev 13:1-2 And I stood upon the sand of the sea, and saw a beast rise up out of the sea, having seven heads and ten horns, and upon his horns ten crowns, and upon his heads the name of blasphemy. And the beast which I saw was like

unto a **leopard**, and his feet were as the feet of a **bear**, and his mouth as the mouth of a **lion**: and the dragon gave him his power, and his seat, and great authority.

And there he is! The Leopard-Bear-Lion Beast of Revelation thirteen (LBL). Notice that this one beast looks like all three of those old empires rolled into one. So what has tied the three separate Middle Eastern states of Iraq, Iran, and Syria together during the last two thirds of the Christian Era? Islam and the false prophet, Muhammad, that's what! Though they have sometimes battled each other, for thirteen centuries Iraq, Iran, Syria and associates, including Saudi Arabia, have been the home of the radical Moslems, the lair of assassins, a haven for terrorists and a roost for all who hate Israel and the Christian nations.

That's not guesswork theology, folks. The Islamic states have historically been the enemies of the West and they still are today. Furthermore, those radical Moslem states will continue to be enemies of God's people until Jesus returns. Why? Well, notice who empowers those countries, the dragon! And Satan has always been the implacable enemy of God and of God's children. Do not be deluded that the Moslem god, Allah, is the same as our Heavenly Father. Our Sovereign God is a God of *love*, a word conspicuously absent from the Koran. There may indeed be loving Moslems, but the Koran doesn't teach it.

So the Leopard-Bear-Lion is Syria-Iraq-Iran, and their radical Islamic friends. But now we need to know when this beast will be in power, and to establish that, we need a little review:

Rev 11:2   But the court which is without the temple leave out, and measure it not; for it is given unto the Gentiles: and the holy city shall they tread under foot forty *and* two months.

The 42 months of Rev 11:2 were explained at length in Chapter 5. They were 1278.34 years, and it was 1278.34 years from the construction of the Dome of the Rock until Jerusalem

GRAPH NUMBER 15

The Beasts of Daniel

Dan 7:3-24 (excerpts) And four great beasts came up from the sea, diverse one from another. The first *was* like a lion, and had eagle's wings: I beheld till the wings thereof were plucked, and it was lifted up from the earth, and made stand upon the feet as a man, and a man's heart was given to it. And behold another beast, a second, like to a bear, and it raised up itself on one side, and *it had* three ribs in the mouth of it between the teeth of it: and they said thus unto it, Arise, devour much flesh. After this I beheld, and lo another, like a leopard, which had upon the back of it four wings of a fowl; the beast had also four heads; and dominion was given to it. After this ... behold a fourth beast, dreadful and terrible, and strong exceedingly; and it had great iron teeth; and it devoured and brake in pieces, and stamped the residue with the feet of it: and it *was* diverse from all the beasts that *were* before it; and it had ten horns ... and, behold, there came up among them another little horn, before whom there were three of the first horns plucked up by the roots: and, behold, in this horn *were* eyes like the eyes of man, and a mouth speaking great things ... Thus he said, The fourth beast shall be the fourth kingdom upon earth, which shall be diverse from all kingdoms, and shall devour the whole earth, and shall tread it down, and break it in pieces. And the ten horns out of this kingdom *are* ten kings *that* shall arise: and another shall rise after them; and he shall be diverse from the first, and he shall subdue three kings

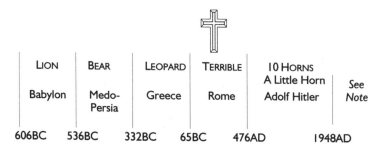

LION	BEAR	LEOPARD	TERRIBLE	10 HORNS A Little Horn	See
Babylon	Medo-Persia	Greece	Rome	Adolf Hitler	Note

| 606BC | 536BC | 332BC | 65BC | 476AD | 1948AD |

NOTE: The Ten Horns of the fourth beast (strong and terrible), arise out of the remnants of the old Roman Empire. Throughout the Christian Era the nations from Roman roots have struggled for world dominion ... the final attempt being made by Adolf Hitler, the "little horn" of Dan 7:8. However, Daniel 7 is not the vision of "ultimate time of the end." Daniel 8 is the end-time vision (Dan 8:19-23), and that vision points to the Leopard-Bear-Lion as the final enemy of the Church and Israel. The Leopard, Bear and Lion beasts had their dominion taken away, but they continued to exist during the Christian Era, and they controlled the Holy Land for "a season and a time" (See graph No. 12 for details).

was again under Jewish control. In the prophecy of the Leopard-Bear-Lion, we again see 42 months (Rev 13:5). LBL was granted authority over Jerusalem for 42 months:

> Rev 13:5 And there was given unto him a mouth speaking great things and blasphemies; and power was given unto him to continue forty *and* two months.

The Leopard-Bear-Lion also was given authority to "blaspheme God's tabernacle" for 42 months, so these prophecies are clearly parallel. They are obviously about the Moslem rule of Jerusalem (688-1967AD). From the above verses we can now positively identify the Leopard-Bear-Lion beast of Revelation 13 as the Moslem states of the Middle East. LBL is not some future antichrist after all. LBL are those Islamic nations that now stand against Israel and the West. Now let's look at Rev 13:3-10 in detail. Explanatory notes are again set within the text, in *italics*:

> Rev 13:3-4 And I saw one of his heads as it were wounded to death [*The battles of Tours and Vienna struck death blows against Moslem expansion into Europe that destroyed their hope of world conquest*]; and his deadly wound was healed [*After WW2, the western nations sent a major portion of their liquid capital into the Middle East which enabled the Moslem states to rebuild*]: and all the world [*Remember that Bible prophecy is ethnographic – The "whole world" refers to the part of the planet John knew about, John's known world. The Lord is not telling us of China, Australia, or the Americas here*] wondered after the beast. And they worshiped the dragon [*This verse shows that Islam is not another route to heaven – The dragon is Satan, ergo, The Moslems worship Satan*] which gave power unto the beast [*LBL*]: and they [*the Moslems*] worshiped the beast, saying, Who *is* like unto the beast? who is able to make war with him? [*During the 1st Jihad the Moslems were indeed victorious over the weaker Christian Middle East and African states and the Eastern Roman Empire*].

> Rev 13:5-6 And there was given unto him a mouth speaking great things and blasphemies; and power was given unto him to continue forty *and* two months. [*the Moslem domination of*

Jerusalem from 688 to 1967 is 42 months of day=years] And he *[LBL, the Moslem states]* opened his mouth in blasphemy against God, to blaspheme his name, and his tabernacle *[The Moslems built a memorial to Muhammad on the footstool of God's feet]*, and them that dwell in heaven *[we dwell in the heavenlies right now, Eph 2:6 "and raised us up with Him, and seated us with Him in the heavenly places, in Christ Jesus"]*.

Rev 13:7-9 And it was given unto him *[LBL]* to make war with the saints, and to overcome them *[The 1st Jihad overwhelmed the Coptic Church which at the time covered the Middle East including North Africa, in fact, from India to Spain]*: and power was given him over all kindreds, and tongues, and nations *[remember that Bible prophecy is ethnographic, that it primarily addresses the countries that surround the Holy land]*. And all that dwell upon the earth shall worship him, whose names are not written in the book of life of the Lamb slain from the foundation of the world *[again a reference to show that Islam is not another road to Heaven]*. If any man have an ear, let him hear.

Rev 13:9-10 He that leadeth into captivity shall go into captivity *[during the 1st Jihad, the area controlled by the Coptic church went into captivity, including the Holy Land]*: he that killeth with the sword must be killed with the sword *[the Moslem armies of the Middle Ages were defeated at Tours and Vienna, with great loss of life]*. Here is the patience and the faith of the saints.

The beasts of Revelation appear to be a figurative picture of Satan's total kingdoms on Earth, both physical and spiritual. The Leopard-Bear-Lion appears to be a VISIBLE aspect of Satan's unseen spiritual kingdom in the Middle East. The Moslems who controlled the Holy Land were held together by a common religion, a spiritual unity, rather than by a common ethnicity. In Rev 13:2, the prophet John also declares the Middle East to be the seat of Satan's power, and Satan's throne does appear to be there.

GRAPH NUMBER 16

Domain of the Leopard-Bear-Lion

Rev 13:1-5 (excerpts) And I ... saw a beast rising up out of the sea having seven heads and ten horns ... And the beast which I saw was like unto a leopard, and his feet were as *the feet* of a bear, and his mouth as the mouth of a lion: and the dragon gave him his power, and his seat, and great authority. And I saw one of his heads as it were wounded to death; and his deadly wound was healed ... And there was given unto him a mouth speaking great things and blasphemies; and power was given unto him to continue forty *and* two months.

Dome of the Rock
688AD

Jerusalem Freed
1967AD

"Authority was given unto him for forty-two months"

Leopard	Bear	Lion
Early Greece	*Medo-Persia*	*Babylon*
now SYRIA	now Iran	now IRAQ

LBL is one beast.
THE ISLAMIC WORLD!

1. "Head slain..." In 732AD, Charles Martel defeated a large Moslem army at the Battle of Tours in southern France. In the Battle of Vienna, 20,000 Christian knights under Jon Sobieski won against 300,000 Moslem cavalrymen. These two battles stopped Moslem incursions into Christian Europe.

2. 42 Months of days = 1278.34 years. 1967 - 1278.34 = 688.66AD, the Dome of the Rock! That is how long LBL beast had "authority" over the Holy City.

THE TEN HORNS OF LBL

There is probably one more aspect of the Leopard-Bear-Lion we ought to examine. When God gave the land of Canaan to Abraham, He set the boundaries thereof: From the River of Egypt (at the southern border of the Gaza Strip) to the River Euphrates (near Damascus in Syria). That area has always been the land the

Lord gave to Isaac and Jacob. The Jews know it and the Arabs know it. But ever since, the Moslems have been trying to take the land God gave to Israel:

> Gen 15:18-21 The LORD made a covenant with Abram, saying, Unto thy seed have I given this land, from the river of Egypt unto the great river, the river Euphrates: The Kenites, and the Kenizzites, and the Kadmonites, And the Hittites, and the Perizzites, and the Rephaims, And the Amorites, and the Canaanites, and the Girgashites, and the Jebusites.

Those peoples were the original inhabitants of the land. When Joshua and the Children of Israel entered Canaan in 1406BC, God commanded them to drive all those people out.[1] They didn't do so. Instead, Israel enslaved the local people and put them to forced labor. When Nebuchadnezzar took the Jews captive to Babylon, he left the "poorer people in the land." That would have included the descendants of those Canaanite slaves, and the descendants of those slaves have been a thorn in the side of Israel ever since. They are probably the Palestinians and they are still a thorn in the side of Israel today![2] But they are only part of the 10 horns.

> *The ten horns of the Leopard-Bear-Lion are the Jihadists like Usama bin Laden with his al Qaeda, Yasser Arafat's Hamas, the Hizbullah, the Islamic Jihad, the PFLP, the Intifada, all the militant fundamental Moslems and the nations that support them: Iraq, Syria, and Iran (in ancient times, Afghanistan bordered the Medo-Persian empire, today's Iran).*

Jews are being tortured and killed almost daily by terrorist Palestinians from the Gaza strip and Jericho, with the full blessing of Yasser Arafat and the surrounding Arab states. The Palestinians are trying to destroy God's people one soul at a time and take their

---

[1] Though the Arabs are also children of Abraham through Hagar, God gave the Holy Land to the people born through Sarah's son Isaac: "Neither, because they are the seed of Abraham, *are they* all children: but, In Isaac shall thy seed be called" (Rom 9:7).

[2] The name Palestinian is derived from Philistine. Those people were the worst of David's enemies. Goliath of Gath was a Philistine.

land one square inch at a time. May Yeshua defend Israel, for no one else will. If an Israeli kills a terrorist in self-defense it is front page in the world's newspapers, reported as a vicious homicide. But if a Palestinian bombs a bus full of women and children, you might find it as a two inch filler, hidden on page 14 of section "B" – and even then, only reported as a justifiable act in a Palestinian "war of liberation" against their Jewish oppressors.

Should we be surprised by this biased journalism? Not at all. That is what we should expect from our media today, considering the influence that OPEC money and Moslem extremists now have on the economies and news agencies of the Western world. Supposedly, these Palestinians are just a poor misunderstood people who are being oppressed by their Jewish landlords, but it isn't so. The Holy Land was a sand hill until, in fulfillment of Scripture, the Jews returned and started cultivating it again:

> Isa 35:1 The wilderness and the solitary place shall be glad for them; and the desert shall rejoice, and blossom as the rose.

A NEWS BRIEF

Christian Action for Israel Newsletter #49, 10/5/2001, 4:55pm

> In Gaza City recently, Palestinians put on a reenactment of the suicide bombing of the Sbarro Pizzeria in Jerusalem. The Palestinian Authority bomber and 15 people were blown to pieces in the actual Aug. 9 bombing. Of the 15 victims, seven were children, including a 4-year-old boy and his 2-year-old sister. One of the victims was a 31-year-old American woman. Four were teen-agers. The exhibition included fake body parts scattered about to add more "realism" to rejoice over.
>
> The Palestinians aren't interested in peaceful coexistence with Israel on any terms. A poll taken last week showed 72 percent of Palestinians favor continuing the uprising, while 66 percent favor continued attacks against Israeli civilians.

Two-Horned Beast

CHAPTER 12

"When will the new moon be over,
so that we may sell grain
and open the wheat market,
to make the bushel smaller and the shekel bigger,
and to cheat with dishonest scales,
so as to buy the helpless for money
and the needy for a pair of sandals."

AMOS 8:4-6 EXCERPTS

FOLLOWING the Leopard-Bear-Lion beast is another great beast: the beast with "Two Horns like a Lamb." Since the 42 months of LBL's dominion take us from 688 to 1967, this later beast might give us information on events that take place AFTER 1967.

Rev 13:11 And I beheld another beast coming up out of the earth; and he had two horns like a lamb, and he spake as a dragon.

Look at how this new beast is described: It is "like a lamb." The Greek word used here for lamb is *arnion*,[1] accurately defined as "a little lambkin." *Arnion* appears 26 times in Revelation, and in every time except this one, *arnion* referred to the "*lamb* of God, which taketh away the sins of the world" (Joh 1:29). So why did the Lord use a lamb to describe this new beast? Because of its nature. This beast will appear to be Christ-like, it will appear to be Christian, but Two-Horns really speaks like the dragon. In other words, this beast would sound just like a Christian empire, but it too would be militant and strongly influenced by Satan.

---

[1] ἀρνίον, Strong's No. G721. arnion, ar-nee'-on; diminutive from G704; a lambkin: lamb.

Now, this beast has two horns. In other words, this empire would have two major kings or kingdoms. These kingdoms might exist at the same time, or from examples like Dan 8:3 and 8:8, they could appear one after the other. So how can we know who these kingdoms are? Well, the Bible doesn't directly state who, but it does tell us when they will rule:

> Rev 13:12 And he exerciseth all the power of the first beast before him [*i.e., in his sight or presence*], and causeth the earth and them which dwell therein to worship the first beast, whose deadly wound was healed.

The Old English of the KJV is a little confusing here, but "before him" in Greek is *enopion,* or "in the sight of."[1] The two-horned beast will rule *in the sight of,* or in the presence of, the Leopard-Bear-Lion beast. Now we already know that LBL was given authority from 688 to 1967. So for this lamb-like beast to rule "in the sight" of LBL, he would have to rule during the *same time.* His two horns would also have to come up between 688 and 1967! That's the key to the identity the Two-Horned Beast, so I'm going to say it again:

> *For the beast with Two Horns like a Lamb to be in the presence of the Leopard-Bear-Lion, he would have to exist while LBL was in power; in other words, his two horns would have to come up between 688 and 1967!*

"In his presence" also means something else. Two Horns and LBL will coexist. Two Horns will not destroy LBL, but will be given authority while LBL remains in the Holy Land. So let's look at the history of the Holy Land, and see if any so-called Christian nations ruled there sometime between 688 and 1967.

The Moslems conquered Jerusalem in 639AD. Forty-nine years later, Abd el Malik Ibn Marwan began construction of the Dome

---

[1] ἐνώπιον, Strong's No. G1799. enopion, en-o'-pee-on; neut. of a comp. of G1722 and a der. of G3700; in the face of (lit. or fig.):--before, in the presence (sight) of, to.

of the Rock on the temple mount. Construction was completed in 705, and Islam ruled victorious in Jerusalem for the next 200 odd years. Satan must have thought it was all over for the Holy Land, the Jews and the Church. The Moslems rejoiced over defeating God's Two Witnesses, a fact that was predicted in the prophecy about them:[1]

> Rev 11:10 (NASB) And those who dwell on the earth will rejoice over them and make merry; and they will send gifts to one another, because these two prophets[*the Two Witnesses*] tormented those who dwell on the earth.

Then in the 10th Century, Pope Urban II called for the Crusades to begin. Christian knights from Europe and England captured Jerusalem and ruled in the Holy Land for the next 200 years. But by the end of the 12th Century, the Crusaders were driven out, and Islam again ruled the country. Moslems continued to rule the Holy Land through several regimes, the final one being the Ottoman Empire.

Though we don't read about it in western histories, the Crusaders raped, murdered, and pillaged the Jews and Arabs who were living in the Holy Land. They claimed to be Christians but they indeed "spoke like the dragon!" They didn't destroy the Dome of the Rock, nor drive the Moslems out of the land so the Crusaders were "in his sight." They were the first horn, and they were in the presence of the Leopard-Bear-Lion!

Seven Centuries later, during World War I, a later group of "Christian knights" again fought against the Islamic world and entered the Holy Land. Lawrence of Arabia and General Allenby (with the blessing of the League of Nations) conquered what was later to be known as the *British Mandate*. The western nations, appearing "like a lamb," ruled in Jerusalem, and from 1917 to

---

[1] A full explanation of the 3 ½ days or Rev 11:9, is contained in a chapter entitled *Hour, Day, Month, and Year*.

GRAPH NUMBER 17

Beast with Two Horns Like a Lamb

Rev 13:11-12 And I beheld another beast coming up out of the earth; and he had two horns like a lamb, and he spake as a dragon. And he exerciseth all the power of the first beast before him, and causeth the earth and them which dwell therein to worship the first beast, whose deadly wound was healed.

Rev 13:13-14 And he doeth great wonders, so that he maketh fire come down from heaven on the earth in the sight of men, And deceiveth them that dwell on the earth by *the means of* those miracles which he had power to do in the sight of the beast; saying to them that dwell on the earth, that they should make an image to the beast, which had the wound by a sword, and did live.

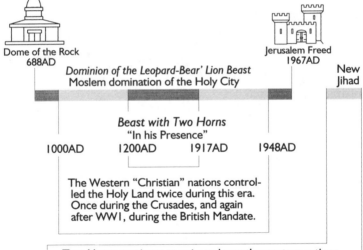

Dome of the Rock
688AD

Jerusalem Freed
1967AD

New Jihad

Dominion of the Leopard-Bear' Lion Beast
Moslem domination of the Holy City

Beast with Two Horns
"In his Presence"

1000AD   1200AD   1917AD   1948AD

The Western "Christian" nations controlled the Holy Land twice during this era. Once during the Crusades, and again after WWI, during the British Mandate.

Two Horns continues to exist today as the western nations. The Beast with "two horns like a Lamb" would appear to be Christian, but speaks like the dragon. In other words, it would be aggressive and ungodly in its behavior. When the "Christian" nations conquered the Holy Land, they did not destroy the Dome of the Rock, nor drive the Moslems out of the land, so they were in the presence of the Leopard-Bear-Lion beast. Today, the western nations are in bondage to Arab oil, so it is Two Horns that is bringing the likeness of the first militant Islam back to life by financing this new Jihad that threatens us all.

The Last Trumpet, 1Co 15:52, Rev 10:7, Rev 11:15

1948, Great Britain controlled the Holy Land. They did not destroy the Dome of the Rock, nor drive the Moslems out. They were another horn "in the sight" of the Leopard-Bear-Lion. Thus, the British Mandate was the second horn of the Two-Horned Beast.

In 1948, the new nation of Israel was established and that ended Gentile domination of the Holy Land, forever. But twice during the 42 months, "Christian nations" did rule in the presence of the Leopard-Bear-Lion, so the western, so-called "Christian" nations are the beast with Two Horns like a Lamb.

THE HEALED BEAST

That takes us to 1948, but that is not the end of the Two-Horned Beast (2H) nor of the Leopard-Bear-Lion:

> Rev 13:12-14   And he [*2H*] exerciseth all the power of the first beast [*LBL*] before him, and causeth the earth and them which dwell therein to worship the first beast [*LBL*], whose deadly wound was healed. And he [*2H*] doeth great wonders, so that he maketh fire come down from heaven on the earth in the sight of men, And deceiveth them that dwell on the earth by *the means of* those miracles which he had power to do in the sight of the [*LBL*] beast.

After World War II, the Beast with Two Horns experienced an accelerated growth in its economies and industry. With western oil fields insufficient for its needs, Two Horns turned to the Middle East. Over the next five decades, a major portion of western hard currency flowed into the coffers of the Leopard-Bear-Lion. Those Middle Eastern nations then used those funds to rebuild Islam and to buy modern weaponry from the West. The Beast with Two Horns "healed" the beast who had a wound of the sword, and Leopard-Bear-Lion came back to life! So for the first time since the Battle of Vienna, radical Islamic states can again threaten the peace of Israel and the Western world.

Indeed, the Beast with Two-Horns "performs great signs" which deceive men and turn their eyes from God. The western nations are the most scientifically advanced on earth. If you had been standing on the streets of Baghdad in 1991 or in Kabul this year, the phrase, "and he even makes fire come down out of Heaven to the earth in the presence of men," wouldn't have been a mystery to you. American guided missiles and smart-bombs are indeed a "fire from Heaven" that is visible to all.

We have dived to the bottom of the bottomless sea, harnessed the atom, sent probes beyond our solar system, and placed men on the Moon. These are great signs which deceive us into thinking man is God (2Th 2:4).

IMAGE OF THE BEAST

There has probably been as much written about the image and mark of the beast as about any other passage in the Bible (Rev 13:14-18). It has always been assumed that this "image of the beast" was something physical, like a statue that was carved, cast, or sculpted out if stone, wood, or metal. But that is not all the dictionary says an image can be.[1]

An image is a likeness of any kind. A photograph is an "image" of the original scene, a book is an "image" of the thoughts of the writer and a child can be the "image" of his father. If we use that broader definition for "image," then the new Moslem Jihad that faces the West and Israel is an image of the first Jihad. For indeed, this new Islamic threat is just as menacing as the one that came before it.

> Rev 13:14 And he [*the Two-Horned Beast*] deceiveth them that dwell on the earth by *the means of* those miracles which he had power to do in the sight of the beast [*LBL*]; saying to them that dwell on the earth, that they should make an image to the [*LBL*] beast [*a likeness of, or a new Islamic power*], which had the wound by a sword, and did live.

---

[1] Image: A duplicate, counterpart, or other representative reproduction of an object. One that closely or exactly resembles another, a double. A mental picture of something that is not real or present.

An image is a likeness, and now a likeness of the first Moslem Jihad is springing up all over the world. The fastest growing religion in Europe is Islam, and as of this writing, the largest mosque in the Western world is in Rome. The largest place of worship in Toronto, Canada, is a mosque, and there are more people attending mosques in England than there are going into the Church of England. In Holland, state-owned Christian churches are now being turned over to Moslems, and 14% of the immigrants into the United States are Islamic.

There are over 1.2 billion or so people in that false religion today. Best estimates are that 10-15 percent of all Moslems are militant fundamental extremists. In other words, 100 to 150 million human beings are in the world's most dangerous splinter group. Since there are an estimated three to five million Moslems here in the United States, if that 10-15% statistic holds true for us, we could reasonably conclude that between 300,000 and 750,000 Moslems in America also support the terrorists.

It is considered an outrageous sin for a Moslem to betray a fellow Moslem to an infidel, regardless of the crime. As a result, extremists can comfortably hide in any Moslem population. They do so right here in this country.

> Dan 8:25 ... he shall cause craft to prosper in his hand; and he shall magnify *himself* in his heart, and by peace shall destroy many:

We are being taken for fools. Did you know that the major portion of Hamas' funding comes from this country? That money isn't being given to the Palestinian terrorists by the tooth fairy.

While claiming to be our friends, these same Moslems, are killing many thousands of Christians in Nigeria, over 1,000,000 Christians in the Sudan – many by crucifixion – thousands more in Indonesia, the Philippines, and anywhere else in the world where there are large Islamic populations. Have we already forgotten our own embassies in Teheran and Africa, the Achille Lauro, Pan Am

107, the Marine barracks in Beirut, Somalia,[1] the first World Trade Center attack and the USS Cole?

So what are the differences between the United States and Nigeria, the Sudan, and Indonesia? Many, but there is one central difference – there are a lot more Moslems in those troubled countries. And what do we hear, even from the President of the United States? That Islam is love and peace. Maybe now we can hear three verses from within the Bowls of Wrath:

> Rev 16:12-14 And the sixth angel poured out his vial upon the great river Euphrates [*which flows between Iraq and Iran*]; and the water thereof was dried up [*as the waters that separated them were figuratively dried up, they figuratively became one land, and through Islam they have spiritually become one people*], that the way of the kings of the east [*LBL*] might be prepared [*Afghanistan is also East of LBL*]. And I saw three unclean spirits [*Leopard-Bear-Lion is a three-part empire*] like frogs *come* out of the mouth of the dragon, and out of the mouth of the beast, and out of the mouth of the false prophet [*Muhammad*]. For they are the spirits of devils, working miracles, *which* go forth unto the kings of the earth and of the whole world [*for the first time in history, Islam is now spreading into the Western world*], to gather them to the battle of that great day of God Almighty.

Note the location of this prophecy: the River Euphrates, a river that runs between Iran and Iraq and into Syria. That's the lair of the Leopard-Bear-Lion once again. Notice how many evil spirits like frogs there are: THREE and LBL beast is a composite three-part beast. It is the release of these three demons into the world that will trigger Armageddon. Just watch how Islam is spreading. The Two-Horned Beast helps the Leopard-Bear-Lion to gain strength to its own harm:

---

[1] There is now credible evidence that Osama bin Laden funded and sent al Queda fighters into Somalia to fight the US Special Forces there, 18 of whom were killed with 75 wounded. Al Queda forces fired from behind the local women and children making it extremely difficult for US troops to defend themselves without causing great collateral damage.

Rev 13:15-16 And he [2H] had power to give life unto the image of the [LBL] beast, that the image [or *likeness*] of the [first LBL] beast should both speak, and cause that as many as would not worship the image of the beast should be killed.

But all of that is far away, and Islam could never be a danger here, right? Yeah right! Most thought so until the World Trade Center fell. But by then, Islam was already a major force among the Black youth in America and many prison populations are controlled by Black Muslims. Of the immigrants now entering this country, 14% are Islamic and Moslems are spending over $1,000,000 a week here to subvert our people. Even as we write, Islamic fundamentalists hold secret meetings in such unlikely places as Tampa, Los Angeles, Oklahoma City, and Kansas City to plot terrorist acts against our nation[1]

But despite the destruction of the World Trade Center, western nations, including our own, still favor Arab interests above those of our staunchest friend in the Middle East, Israel. Ignoring the fact that Yasser Arafat and his henchman, Abu Abas, invented airplane hijacking, the Palestinians still have access to the highest echelons of our government. We listen, in a vain attempt to further a peace process that will never work. Arafat is the most murderous terrorist who ever lived, yet we demand that Israel make peace with him. You cannot make peace with those intent on your obliteration, and though it hasn't happened yet, the Bible indicates that our listening to the Leopard-Bear-Lion could lead to the destruction of the Church in the Western world:

Rev 11:7 And when they shall have finished their testimony, the beast that ascendeth out of the bottomless pit shall make war against them, and shall overcome them, and kill them.

That death may be physical, but surely it is spiritual, as the Church stumbles about in a self-induced doctrinal trance. At no time since

[1] M. Ali, *Christianity's Greatest Challenge* (Kaduna, Nigeria, Soul Winning Team Ministries) pp. 2-5

the Reformation has the Church known less about Jesus or the Bible than it does right now. Blinded by tradition, lethargy, and the cares of this world, we keep right on playing. In Matthew 24:25 the Lord promised He would tell us all this in advance, and He has. But Jesus will still be returning as a thief, for few there are who await His appearing.

GRAPH NUMBER 18

Summary of Day-Years & Times

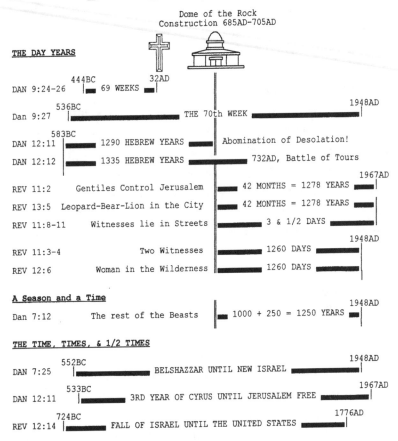

NOTE: Thirteen day=year historic fits are too many to ignore. The mathematical and historic evidence for his method of interpretation is overwhelming.

The Big Lie

CHAPTER 13

*And he shall destroy
the mighty and the holy people,
and through his policy also
he shall cause craft to prosper in his hand;
and by peace shall destroy many.*

Dan 8:24-25

With full permission of the author, M. Ali, all Koranic quotes and all the information about Muhammad and Islam is directly quoted from *Islam Reviewed, 2nd American Edition* (Fish House Publishing, Fort Myers FL, 1999). M. Ali is a well educated former Moslem who is now a Christian and an evangelist to Moslems.

IF we listen to the American media, President Bush and other politicians, we hear that this isn't a religious war, that Islam is peace, and even love. It is a big lie. From openly biased Islamic professors in our universities, we also hear that the United States' war on the terrorist groups in Afghanistan is unjustified. That's another big lie – talking heads trying to lull the American people asleep to the hidden danger that faces us. It isn't hijacked planes or potential bio-chemical attacks that we need to worry about, but fundamental Islam itself.

It is significant that President Bush didn't name the terrorist organizations in Israel and that Colin Powell, the US Secretary of State, continually pressures Israel to implement a so-called "peace process" with terrorist groups. The reason, of course, is to keep the petroleum rich Islamic states from shutting off our oil supply. A pragmatic policy, perhaps, but morally bankrupt.

Yasser Arafat and his associates, the Hamas, the Islamic Jihad, the PFLP and the Palestinian Authority are continually being implicated in the every-day shootings and bombings taking place in Israel – women and children being murdered by snipers. Despite the public face Arafat shows to the West, his many speeches in Arab states call for the complete destruction of Israel. If you question the validity of that statement, just go to Arutz Sheva, http://www.israelnationalnews.com or read any other less Arab biased newspaper.

The Iranian and Syrian sponsored Hizbollah (Party of Allah) bombard northern Israel with rocket-propelled grenades and artillery, and they continually set ambushes and booby traps for Israeli soldiers. Philip Schaff, in writing on the history of the Christian church, clearly states the Islamic mind-set:

"The Sword", says Muhammad "is the key of heaven and hell; a drop of blood shed in the cause of Allah, a night spent in arms, is of more avail than two months of fasting and prayer; whoever falls in battle, his sins are forgiven, and at the day of judgment his limbs shall be supplied by the wings of angels and cherubim." This was the secret of his success. Idolaters had to choose between Islam, slavery and death; Jews and Christians were allowed to purchase a limited toleration by the payment of Jizya (humility tax), but were nonetheless kept in degrading bondage ... The khalifs, Muhammad's successors who like him united the priestly and kingly divinity, carried on his conquests with the battle cry: "Before you is paradise, behind you are death and hell." Inspired by the weakness of the Byzantine empire and the internal distraction of the Greek church, the wild sons of the desert who were content with the plainest food, and disciplined in the school of war, hardship and recklessness of life, subdued Palestine, Syria and Egypt, embracing the classical soil of primitive Christianity. Thousands of Christian churches in the patriarchal diocese of Jerusalem, Antioch and Alexandria were ruthlessly destroyed or converted into mosques. Twenty years after Muhammad's death, the crescent ruled over a realm as large as the Roman Empire.

The command to fight for the cause of Allah is given in many Suras of the Koran:

"Then fight in the cause of God and know that God heareth and knoweth all things" (Sura 2:244).

The command to fight relentlessly is given in Sura 4:74. In Sura 8:65, Allah encouraged Muhammad to incite Moslems to fight. Listen to Allah giving the Jihad order:

"But when the forbidden months are past, then fight and slay the pagans wherever ye find them, and seize them, beleaguer them and lie in wait (ambush) for them in every stratagem (of war) but if they repent, and establish regular prayers and practice regular charity, then open the way for them: for God is oft-forgiving most merciful" (Sura 9:5).

"O ye who believe! fight the unbelievers ... " (Sura 9:123).

Those who are ignorant of the Koran and Islam are astonished when they hear about Islam's slaughtering of Christians, but Moslems are just doing what they think is right. Allah specifically commands Moslems to fight against Christians and Jews until they are reduced to a condition worse than slaves:

"Fight those who believe not in God [*Allah*] and his apostle [*Muhammad*], nor acknowledge the religion of truth [*even if they are*] of the people of the book [*i.e. Jews and Christians*], until they pay jizya [*humiliating tax*] with willing submission, and feel themselves subdued [*enslaved*]" (Sura 9:29).

In obedience to Allah's call to fight, Muhammad spent a great deal of his own time between the Hijra (flight) and his death mapping out strategies for the purpose of spreading Islam, personally getting involved in ambushes and other battles. Islamic historians themselves confirm that Muhammad was present at twenty six such armed conflicts and fought actively in nine (Risalatu Abdullah & C., 47, CF. Ibn Hisham Vol. 3, P. 78).

Many try to explain away the high level of terrorism perpetrated by various Islamic groups, but all recognize Jihad as part of today's reality. Enthusiastically employed as a means of propagating Islam during the dark ages, Jihad now embarrasses many moderate Moslems. But despite the views of moderate Islamic governments, if fundamentalism becomes the dominant belief of their people, those governments will either agree to fundamentalist demands or those governments will fall. The ousting of the Shah of Iran is a good example.

Faithful Moslems have been drumming Islam's militant agenda for decades, but the West didn't think it needed to worry.[1] Before Israel even became a state, Ayatollah Khomeini was going into all the Islamic colleges, theological seminaries and schools in Iran, teaching them a five point agenda:

Stage 1: Iran must become a theocratic, fundamentalist Islamic State.

Stage 2: Iraq must become a theocratic, fundamentalist Islamic State.

Stage 3: Saudi Arabia, Jordan, Syria, Egypt, have to become fundamentalist, theocratic Islamic States.

Stage 4: Jerusalem must be retaken and the Jewish people destroyed.

Stage 5: Conquest of the nations.

As recent history shows, Stage 1 has been accomplished and there is no Moslem, fundamentalist or moderate, who does not also believe in stages 4 and 5. That is so important, I must say it again: *There is no Moslem, fundamentalist or moderate, who does not also believe in stages 4 and 5.* Those five stages are bonds that unite all Moslems, regardless of sect or geographic location. Let's say it again, Islam's ambitions are:

(1) Annexation of Jerusalem and annihilation of the Jews
(2) Obliteration of Christianity
(3) Conquest of all nations.

---

[2] In a 3/22/99 speech delivered in Egypt, Hillary Clinton, wife of the former American president, declared that the United States would be more accepting of Islam in the future. Total insanity! If fundamental Islam ever gains political control in the United States, individual freedom and freedom of worship will be a thing of the past, just as it is in most Islamic states today.

To most Moslems, the failure to achieve those objectives means the failure of Islam and consequently, the failure of Allah – an unimaginable blasphemy to them. Islam will never renounce its claim to Jerusalem, neither will it relent in its effort to destroy the Jews. In 1984, Ayatollah Khomeini declared to the entire world:

> "In order to achieve the victory of Islam in the world, we need to provoke repeated crises, restored value to the idea of death and martyrdom. If Iran has to vanish, that is not important. The important thing is to engulf the world in crises. Those who are called to export the revolution will lose their unhealthy desire for comfort and will attain the maturity needed to fulfill their mission. The road to Jerusalem goes through Kerbala." (an Iraqi town)[1]

These are not the words of a naive, overwrought, emotional fanatic with stone-age ideas, as the West mistakenly concludes. Ayatollah Khomeini was one of the most politically astute theological minds in the Islamic world. He was able to perfectly express the mind of Allah and Islam, and though he has been long dead, his manifesto lives on. One prays that United States political thinkers will heed what is written here, but the government is now so politically and morally compromised, that any departure from a policy of appeasing Islam is most unlikely. Blindly optimistic, the American bureaucracy totally ignores the Moslem view of a treaty signed with infidels. In the Moslem mind, any agreement made with an infidel is not binding.

If the Koran is to be accepted at face value, and Muhammad is to be considered to be the model of correct Islamic behavior, those so called "extremists" or "fundamentalists" are actually the true Moslems. Moslems who are hungry for Christian blood are really the ones who are obeying what the Koran says:

> "Therefore when ye meet the unbelievers [*in fight*] smite at their necks; at length, when ye have thoroughly subdued them, bind a bond firmly [*on them*]" (Sura 47:4).

---

[1] Quoted in *Le Point, No. 599*, March 12, 1984, pp. 89-90

The Koran abounds with that type of inflammatory Sura and that is why all true Moslems wish unbelievers dead (especially Christians and Jews). Islam has divided the world into two distinct camps:

1. The *Dar al-Salaam*, i.e. the household of peace.
2. The *Dar al-Harb*, i.e. the household of war.

Everyone who is not a Moslem is in the *Dar al-Harb*. They are regarded as infidels, the enemies of Allah, whose heads may be chopped off at will. Barbaric? Yes indeed, but it's a reality today. There are Christian churches hidden throughout Arabia and beheading is exactly what happens to them if they are ever caught. So let's take a closer look at the "peace-loving" founder of Islam:

Muhammad was born in 570 AD in Mecca (correctly pronounced Makka), a city northwest of Arabia. His father, Abdullah (meaning servant of Allah) died before he was born. His mother, Amia, died when he was six. He was raised, first by his grandfather, Abdul Muttalib, and later by his uncle, Abdul Manaf, also known as Abu Talib. He was of the Hashimite clan of Quraish tribe. As a young boy he traveled with his uncle in merchant caravans to Syria, and for some years after he made similar journeys in the service of a wealthy widow.

At the age of forty-three, Muhammad went to the public square around the Ka'aba stone to preach. He proclaimed that Allah was one, unseen and all-powerful. He condemned the worship of other gods beside Allah and warned of a coming day of judgment. In thirteen years of peaceful preaching, he won about a hundred followers. Persecution broke out and some of his followers fled to Abyssinia (now Ethiopia, a Christian country).

The Negus of Abyssinia and his Christian subjects protected the Moslems and lavished love on them. When the Meccan persecutors demanded their repatriation, the Christians refused to hand them over. The Moslems had earlier defended their faith in public debate, confessing their belief in Christ's virgin birth, His miracles, and His ascension into heaven (the favorable passages about Jesus in the Koran may be there for that reason).

But, Muhammad's accommodation with the Christians was short-lived. After Islam became fully established, it revealed its true colors as a rabid anti-Christian religion, and the blotting out of Christianity from under the sun has been a major aim of Islam ever since. In their quest to destroy Christianity, Moslems even went as far as to forge a false "gospel," allegedly written by Barnabas.[1]

Following in the footsteps of their prophet, Muhammad's successors, the Khalifahs, launched a Jihad against Christendom in Mesopotamia, Asia minor, central Asia, and in Egypt, killing millions and forcing the rest to embrace Islam.[2] Then they attacked and occupied Jerusalem. As if all this wasn't enough, on the very site where the magnificent temple of the God of Heaven once stood, the Moslems chose to construct the Dome of the Rock and their third most "holy" mosque, the Al-Aqsa Mosque. Why was the Dome placed where it was, if not to desecrate the temple site of the God of the Bible?

The Moslems undid most of what the early apostles had achieved in the Middle East by invading Christian populated North Africa, murdering many and forcing the rest to Islam at the point of the sword. Even today it is a crime to preach Christ in most Middle Eastern countries. As stated earlier, in Arabia, if a Saudi national is found to be a Christian, he is beheaded.

The battle-hardened Islamic "missionaries" then swept over Palestine, drove on to Persia, continued their drive into northwest India, and settled finally on the southern steps of Russia. They overran Spain and invaded France. Thank God for Charles Martel

---

[1] Barnabas is believed to have been written by a monk named Marino, a Catholic turned Moslem, who was later known as Mustapha Arandi. Barnabas contains direct quotes from the Koran and from a 15th century comedy by Dante.

[2] Before his death in 632, Muhammad ordered a military operation against Christian Byzantine (the Eastern Roman Empire).

who halted their advance into Europe. But for that battle, Islam could have overrun the entire continent. Islam is now using their petrol dollars to achieve what they could not accomplish earlier through the sword. Through its control of oil, Islam is now expanding at the expense of Christendom.

IMPORTANT DATES IN ISLAMIC CONQUEST:

632 AD – Islamic Jihadists conquered Yemen.

632 AD – Invasion of Abyssinia (Ethiopia) but the invading Islamic army was repelled by the orthodox church backed by the Portugese. This was a particularly disgraceful event, because just seventeen years earlier, Abyssinia had helped the persecuted Moslems.

633 AD – All the desert tribes of Arabia were thoroughly subdued through military campaigns.

635 AD – The attacking Islamic army conquered Damascus.

637AD – The Persians (Iranians) were defeated at the battle of Qadisiyya.

637 AD – The fall of Iraq

638 AD – Islamic fighters occupied Jerusalem.

639 AD – All of Syria fell into Moslems hands.

642 AD – All of Egypt fell to Moslems after some resistance in Alexandria. The great Coptic church was destroyed never to get strong again.

670 AD – Khalif Muawiya ordered an unsuccessful sea assault against Byzantium.

688 AD – The fall of Carthage.

702 AD – The Berber tribes of North Africa conquered.

705 - 708 AD – Occupation of North Africa.

711-713 AD – Arabian expansionists captured all of Spain and Portugal. The place the Islamic Commander pitched his headquarters still bears his name, Gibralter, in English, or Jebel Tariq (Arabic), meaning mountain of Tariq.

715-717 AD – Arabian armies subdued Afghanistan, central Asia, northern limit of the Caspian sea, much of northern India.

718AD – Islamic forces started attacking France.

725AD – The invading Islamic armies besieged Toulouse and raided Burgundy and the Rhone valley.

732 AD – Bordeaux was besieged. The Islamic armies advanced up to Poitiers where they were defeated by Charles Martel.[1]

And thus, just one century after the death of Muhammad, the domain of Islam stretched from the Pyrenees to the Himalayas, from the Atlantic to the Indian Ocean, and from central Asia to central Africa.

From 750 AD onwards, Islam went through a period of stagnation. For a time, intellectual, commercial and artistic pursuit became more prominent, and by the eleventh century, the Islamic empire was weak enough for the Vatican to venture the crusades. However, this provoked the Moslems to more conquests:

11th Century AD – Moslems penetrated Africa south of the Sahara.

12th - 14th Century AD – Moslems' occupation of northern India.

13th Century AD – A band of Moslem states linked Dakar (Senegal) to the Red Sea across the sub-Sahara prairies.

14th - 16th Century AD – Moslem fighters conquered Indonesia.

15th Century AD – Constantinople falls. That city (renamed Istanbul) was the eastern bastion of the whole of the Christian world. The great Christian church of Santa Sofia built by Christian emperor Justinian, was then turned into a mosque.

---

[1] CHRONICLE OF ST. DENIS: The Moslems planned to go to Tours to destroy the Church of St. Martin, the city, and the whole country. Then came against them the glorious Prince Charles, at the head of his whole force. He drew up his host, and he fought as fiercely as the hungry wolf falls upon the stag. By the grace of Our Lord, he wrought a great slaughter upon the enemies of Christian faith, so that--as history bears witness--he slew in that battle 300,000 men, likewise their king by name Abderrahman. Then was he [Charles] first called "Martel," for as a hammer of iron, of steel, and of every other metal, even so he dashed: and smote in the battle all his enemies. And what was the greatest marvel of all, he only lost in that battle 1500 men. From: William Stearns Davis, ed., *Readings in Ancient History: Illustrative Extracts from the Sources,* 2 Vols. (Boston: Allyn and Bacon, 1912-13), Vol. II: *Rome and the West,* pp. 362-364

1683AD – The Battle of Vienna. Decisive loss for the Moslems and that defeat ended their attempts to take Europe.[1]
1804 AD – Islamic Jihadists conquer northern Nigeria.

ISLAM, A BRIEF HISTORICAL BACKGROUND

Since many western nations have a distorted or vague knowledge of Islam, it is essential to give a brief historical background of this political entity that is also a religion. Islam literally means submission. Consequently a true Moslem is one who submits in every way to the Koran. Islam is not Muhammadanism nor are Moslems Muhammadans. Such terms are a misnomer and quite offensive to Moslems. Islam revolves around a central figure called Muhammad, but that does not mean the religion is built around or on Muhammad. According to Moslems he was only an instrument of Allah.

Islam is not just a religious but a political entity, and since politics is a game of compromise, Muhammad did make concessions to his Arabian opponents. He recognized and worshiped their idols (Al-Lat, Al-Uzza and Manat) (Sura 53:18-22). When these concessions backfired, Muhammad blamed Satan for putting false "revelations" in his mouth (Sura 22:52). These satanic verses (of Salmon Rushdie fame) came in the same way as Muhammad's earlier visions, but he never once suspected that they all might have had the same source.

June 25th, 622 marked the turning point in Islam as Muhammad migrated (Hijra) to Yatrib (now Medina) and was declared as head of state and commander in chief of the first Islamic Umma (community of believers). Moslems start their dating from that year. Thus, according to Islam, we are in the fifteenth

---

[1] One of the greatest battles ever fought against Moslem forces took place at the gates of Vienna, September 12, 1683. Like the Battle of Tours before it, this battle saved Europe from falling to Islam. The city was besieged by a large Islamic force of about 275,000-300,000 Turks and Tartars, led by Grand Vizier Kara Mustafa. Christian forces were losing the battle until Jan Sobieski, King of Poland, entered the field with about 30,000 knights. The Turks left 15,000 dead on the battlefield. Christian losses are believed to have been about 3500 dead and wounded.

century, not the twentieth. Moslems also ignore the Sabbath. That Satan would attempt to change time and days is stated in black and white in Daniel 7:25:

"He will speak against the most high and oppress his saints and try to change the set time and laws ..." (NIV)

Once Muhammad had consolidated his position in Medina, his god, Allah, commanded him to wage a Jihad. Attacks and counter attacks continued until a ten year peace pact was signed with the Meccans, known as the treaty of Al-Hudaybiyah. This treaty was just a ploy, and Muhammad invaded Mecca two years later at the head of ten thousand fanatical Jihadists (cf. Daniel 11:23-24). Realizing that any resistance would be suicidal, the Meccans surrendered unconditionally.

Muhammad's bitter enemies, Abu Sufyan, Suhail and the like, saved their lives by immediately switching over to Islam. Those who would not do so were summarily executed (Another sterling example of Allah's tender mercies). Since then, Islam has maintained a steady expansion throughout the Third World, most of it by open military aggression.

And Islam has not changed in modern times. Though we tend to ignore them, their attacks continue. In 1992, the U.N. Security Council imposed an air travel and arms embargo on Libya. This action was taken because Libya refused to hand over the two men who were implicated in the blowing up of the Pan-Am passenger plane over Lockerbie, Scotland, a 1988 terrorist act in which 270 people were killed. Because the perpetrators were Moslems and in the *Dar al-Salaam*, Libya hid them for years, until international pressure made it impossible for them to continue doing so.

On Tuesday 5th and Friday 8th May 1992, Radio France International reported the death of fifty people as Islamic fundamentalists attacked Coptic Christians in Egypt. The attacks against Coptic Christians continue to this day. Later that year, the

Islamic Salvation Front of Algeria asked its members to take up arms against its own government, a conflict that is ongoing.

In 1996, radical Taliban Moslems in Afghanistan captured Kabul with the intent of setting up a fundamental Islamic state based on strict Koranic law. They have done so, putting in place one of the most degrading to women and oppressive governments that exists on the planet today.

Fundamental Moslems in the Sudan have slaughtered over 2,000,000 unarmed villagers, both Christian and animists. Christian pastors are routinely crucified. Christian women have their breasts cut off, making it impossible for them to feed their babies who subsequently starve to death. The West has known about this genocide for years, but little has been done to stop it.[1]

The following is an eyewitness decade-long synopsis of what is happing in one predominately Christian country, Nigeria:

We don't need to go to the historical archives to find out what Jihad is like. Moslems regularly slaughter Christians here, and at random. Here are a few examples:

In the North, with the full backing of local authorities, Churches are pulled down at will. The excuse? The North is now an Islamic State. M. Ali, the author of *Islam Reviewed* was in Kano in 1980, when an Islamic riot broke out, killing 4,177 people (official figure) with millions of dollars worth of properties destroyed. In October 1982, the Islamic faithful were again

---

[1] Until this very year, the United States tacitly supported the Christian people in southern Sudan, but the present Bush administration has shifted the support of the US to the Moslem north, probably to strengthen our coalition with the Islamic states. However, in so doing, we put this country on the side of genocidal mass butchers as evil as any in Nazi Germany. Reported on Marlon Maddox Radio Talk Show, *Point of View*, 2:30pm, 10/17/2001. The hypocrisy and gross immorality of such a policy is beyond comprehension. There is a righteous God in heaven who will not long defend those countries that support the murderers of His people.

destructive, setting eight big churches ablaze. In that same year, the Moslems in Kaduna went berserk, slaying 400 people (official figure).

In 1984, Islamic fury erupted in Yola and Jimeta, killing 700 people, including some policemen, and rendered 5,913 people homeless. In March 1987, Moslems in Kaduna, Zaria, Kafanchan and Katsina launched a half-week Jihad against Christians. In Zaria alone, all one hundred big churches were fire-bombed. Several Christians were butchered and many others were roasted to death. Many known Christian buildings were destroyed. In all those cities, any motor vehicle that displayed a Christian sticker was attacked.

In April 1991, Moslems in Bauchi went on an indiscriminate killing spree, burning down churches and destroying a great deal of personal property. About 350 people were killed.

On October 14th 1991, the Moslems in Kano went on rampage again, ostensibly to disrupt a crusade during which the German-born evangelist, Reinhard Bonnke, was to preach. They planned to murder Bonnke himself. It is difficult to arrive at the exact casualty figure there, because many of the murdered Christians were dumped into wells. However, it is estimated that over 2,000 Christians were cut down by Islamic swords. In this case, however, the Moslems, too, suffered casualties:

"Unlike previous religious riots in which non-indigenes (the non-violent) and Christians turned the other cheek or ran for their lives, this time they hit back. Within hours of the fundamentalists unleashing a reign of terror, the non-indigenes mobilized themselves into a militia force, brandishing cutlasses, matchets, iron rods and broken bottles in a counter attack."[1]

In May 1992, Zangon-Kataf, a town about 200 km south of Kaduna was destroyed, the Moslem settlers clashing with the indigenous church-going Kataf. The entire town was devastated

---

[1] Page 16 of the Oct. 28, 1991 edition of Newswatch Magazine

and farmlands destroyed. The destruction was so total that federal authorities declared it a disaster area.

Within a few days, the war spread to Kaduna. The Moslem plan was to attack Christians during their Sunday worship services. They struck at 8 PM, local time, slaughtering people from house to house, chanting "Allahu Akbar" as they went. Many churches were set ablaze, and as usual, other Christian buildings were targeted. Thousands perished.

On September 14, 1994, the Islamic faithfuls struck Potiskum, Yobe State (North East Nigeria), killing three people including an ECWA church Pastor, Yahaya Tsalibi, who was conducting communion service. Nine churches were set ablaze and millions of dollars worth of property was destroyed (Police estimate).

In Kano, on December 26, 1994, Mr. Gideon Akaluka (a Christian) was beheaded by a mob of Moslem faithful, allegedly for defiling a portion of the Koran. They paraded around the city with his severed head on a pole, chanting a victory slogan.

In Sokoto, northwest Nigeria, another Christian was mercilessly beaten because a Moslem beggar who was asking for alms accused him of insulting the prophet. Mr. Azubuike was more fortunate than most; he was thought dead and abandoned.

July 1-7, 1995, Moslems attacked Sayawa Christian community of Tafawa Balewa, Bauchi State (northeast Nigeria). The Moslems then proceeded to attack and burn down 30 Christian villages. Over 1,000 homes were razed. Christians were killed by the thousands. Seventy-seven churches were burned to the ground. Properties worth millions were destroyed. Not even women and children were spared in this genocidal Jihad – the Islamic faithful slaughtering 36 women and children who had taken refuge at a church building in another village. The women even had their bellies ripped open. In another village called Bununu, in Bula district, twenty-two school children (ages 11 to 16 years) were trapped and butchered by Moslems.

Wouldn't you think the police or military would come to the rescue of these defenseless people? Not a chance, and no Moslem ever stood before a court of law to answer for the numerous acts of vandalism, not to mention the countless murders they committed. Instead, the Christian victims of that Jihad had to stand trial before a military tribunal for causing the trouble. A gross miscarriage of justice? Certainly, but eventually one becomes accustomed to the ever-present threat of governmental injustice or Moslem violence. So accustomed to it, in fact, that we just started calling it the "Nigerian Factor."

The religious fervor that caused above atrocities is not going to go away. Authorities who think they can appease Moslems by supporting them against Christians need a better understanding of Islamic law. According to the Koran, true Moslems cannot be appeased until a pure, non-negotiable, Islamic government with a Sharia, i.e., fundamental Islamic constitution is in force in the nation where they live.[1]

Even worse than the atrocities is the apathy of the church towards Moslem evangelism, for the problem lies not with a people who are worse than any other. It lies in the religious system they have been taught and they so earnestly believe. As long as Moslems believe the Koran to be of God, they will continue to burn, rape, and murder their opponents.

We have ignored the irreconcilable spiritual differences that exist between ourselves and Islam. The Moslem goal first, last and always, has been to conquer the world for Islam by the power of

---

[1] Editor's Note: That's not just Nigerian secular authorities, but governments anywhere who try come to some diplomatic accord with Moslem fundamentalists, Palestinians included. By true Islamic law, it is not only permissible but laudable to lie, cheat, steal and even murder those who are not Moslems. After all, they are infidels and in the House of War. As a result, Islamic militants will not depart from their stated intent of destroying Israel and the United States just because of some worthless paper they signed but have no intention of honoring. The liberal media in the West blindly applauds such agreements as wonderful "peace initiatives," but the non-Islamic nations will eventually pay a staggering price for failing to understand the true nature of Islam.

the sword. It won't be long before the Jihad they live with in Israel, Indonesia, the Philippines, North Africa and Europe reaches its bloody sword across the Atlantic, and the West suffers for its diplomatic folly.[1]

Jos, Nigeria, 10/29/2001

Dear Brother Skolfield,

Moslems launched a devastating attack on our city after their Friday Jummat prayer. We managed to escape by God's grace, but we have been living like refugees for the past eleven days. No place is really safe. Just yesterday we heard that Moslems secretly killed a number of college students. Things are so bad now that we sleep with one eye open.

We sympathize with you, the brethren and the entire U.S. over the Islamic Jihadists suicide attack on Washington and New York. Your book is becoming clearer by the day yet the devil is stigmatizing the church against hearing it.

Your brother in the Lord.
M. Ali

(Author of Islam Reviewed)

---

[1] Editor's Note: The wealthy Arabian terrorist, Osama bin Laden, stated publically that he would explode two nuclear devices in the United States in the year 2000 as his part in the ever-expanding Islamic Jihad against the West. That he and all fundamental Islam are at war with the West is patently obvious. Well, bin Laden missed his declared deadline, but as of this writing, his organization was able to hijack four planes in 2001, two of which destroyed the World trade Center and one that damaged the Pentagon. US intelligence agencies had already implicated bin Laden in two US embassy bombings, the battle in Somalia and the attack on the USS Cole, but the Clinton administration did little to stop him.

Scarlet Beast

CHAPTER 14

And the light of a candle shall shine
no more at all in thee;
and the voice of the bridegroom and of the bride
shall be heard no more at all in thee...
And in her was found the blood of prophets,
and of saints,
and of all that were slain upon the earth.

REV 18:23-24

HISTORICALLY positioned at the fall of the Davidic kingdom, Daniel's visions accurately predict the four great Gentile empires, who would rule in the Holy Land during the Time of the Gentiles. The visions of the "Great Image" and "Four Beasts" identify those major Middle Eastern empires as Babylon, Medo-Persia, Greece, and Rome (Daniel chapters 2 and 7). The descendants of those empires, united under Islam, continued to rule the Holy Land from 639 to 1948-1967.

Daniel's primary ministry was to tell the Jews about their future during the 2573 years their land would be under Gentile control, and he did so in a series of parallel and repetitive prophecies. The Lord also told Daniel how long that Gentile domination would last (the Time, Times, and a half), but Daniel couldn't understand *"time"* (Dan 12:8), so until this generation, nobody knew when the Time of the Gentiles would be over.

After the cross, God inspired another apocalyptic prophet, the Apostle John, to write the book of Revelation. John was positioned at the beginning of the Christian Era, and his book is primarily about this era.[1] The Leopard-Bear-Lion identifies the Islamic beast who would trespass on the Holy City for 1278 years, while the Scarlet Beast is an overview of the Gentile empires that would trouble God's people throughout time.

> Rev 17:3 So he carried me away in the spirit into the wilderness: and I saw a woman sit upon a scarlet coloured beast, full of names of blasphemy, having seven heads and ten horns.

When we look back at history through the grid of Revelation, the seven heads of Rev 17:3 exactly fit the world empires that have controlled the Holy Land down through the ages. But to understand who these empires are, we need to look at them from the historic position of the Apostle John, in about 100AD:

> Rev 17:10-11 And there are seven kings: five are fallen, and one is, and the other is not yet come; and when he cometh, he must continue a short space.

During John's lifetime, Rome was in power, so Rome was empire number six, the empire that IS. The "five fallen" would then have to be five empires that controlled the Holy Land before John's time. Four of those empires can easily be documented as Assyria, Babylon, Medo-Persia and Greece. The identity of the first

---

[1] Revelation is also a figurative work, and it is organized in exactly the same way that Daniel is – in a series of repetitive prophecies. The two beasts of Revelation 13 and 17 are repetitive pictures of world history, and they are repeated in an organized way. Rev 17 equals Rev 13 as the B=B of Rev's 2nd chiasm. The chiasm is a Hebrew poetic form that was used in both Daniel and Revelation. The chapter Chiasms & Bifids in *Sozo, Survival Guide for a Remnant Church* explains this form and shows how it is key to understanding the parallel and repetitive nature of the visions in the apocalyptic books. If there is sufficient interest in this book, a sequel will be released that contains all this supporting information.

"king" is less certain; it could be Egypt, but it is more probably the Canaanites.[1]

A 7th empire would follow Rome and continue a little while. After Rome fell in 476AD, the next major empire to rule in the Holy Land was the Leopard-Bear-Lion, and in God's eternal eyes, the Moslems did remain a little while. 1260 years is a "short space" for an eternal God.[2]

The seven heads of the Scarlet Beast are human empires that existed in both Old and New Testament eras, so who is the beast itself? The Scarlet Beast out of which those heads came must have existed for thousands of years. No human empire lasts through millennia, so this beast must be some unseen creature or kingdom that has existed in the spiritual world for thousands of years. And it has! This Scarlet Beast has been influencing the empires of men of every age, and those kingdoms were given into his hand long ago, just as the Bible told us at the temptation of Jesus:

---

[1] Some teach that the seven kings of the Scarlet Beast were Roman emperors of the 1st century and that Revelation was primarily written to the Church of John's time. However, we can now conclusively prove that the Two Witnesses, the Leopard-Bear-Lion, and the day=years are repetitive prophecies that span the Christian Era. Consequently, it is hermeneutically unsound to conclude that out of the whole book of Revelation, only Chapter 17 would be addressed to the Church of the 1st Century. If Rev 17 was only to the 1st century Church, it would be a departure from the repetitive chiastic pattern the Lord revealed through the prophet Daniel. For details, see the chapter on Chiasms & Bifids in *Sozo, Survival Guide for a Remnant Church*.

[2] Nazi Germany geographically duplicated the old Roman Empire, and it lasted for a very "short space" (just 12 years), so I wrote in *Hidden Beast 2* that Nazi Germany was probably the 7th head of the Scarlet Beast. I was wrong! Since a "short space" is a rather vague term, I was looking at that space of time from man's perspective rather than God's. That "short space" probably means something like, "I'm going to the store, and I'm going to stay there for a short space," indicating that I am going to spend some time at the store. When the Lord declared that the 7th head would continue "for a short space," it now appears He was declaring that the Leopard-Bear-Lion Beast would rule in the Holy Land for 1260 years, just as the day=years and time, times have now shown us.

GRAPH NUMBER 19

Seven Heads of the Scarlet Beast

Rev 17:8 (KJV)   The beast that thou sawest was, and is not; and shall ascend out of the bottomless pit, and go into perdition: and they that dwell on the earth shall wonder, whose names were not written in the book of life from the foundation of the world, when they behold the beast that was, and is not, and yet is.

Rev 17:10 (KJV)   And there are seven kings: five are fallen, and one is, *and* the other is not yet come; and when he cometh, he must continue a short space. And the beast that was, and is not, even he is the eighth, and is of the seven, and goeth into perdition.

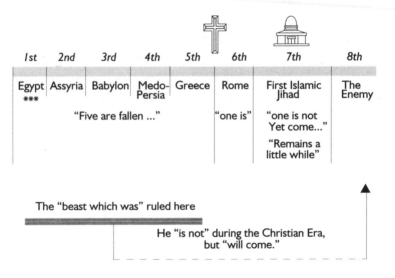

1st	2nd	3rd	4th	5th	6th	7th	8th
Egypt ***	Assyria	Babylon	Medo-Persia	Greece	Rome	First Islamic Jihad	The Enemy
	"Five are fallen ..."				"one is"	"one is not Yet come..."	
						"Remains a little while"	

The "beast which was" ruled here

He "is not" during the Christian Era, but "will come."

NOTE: To understand this prophecy, stand in the historic position of the prophet. It was given to John in 95AD, so Rome was the kingdom that "is "! The five "that are fallen" were kingdoms that existed before John. Kingdoms seven and eight have to come after John. Since Rev 17 speaks primarily of the Gentile nations that dominated the Holy Land throughout time, the 7th head is probably the Moslem powers that controlled Jerusalem between 688 and 1967.

*** Though Egypt had considerable influence over the land of Canaan prior to Joshua's invasion, Scripture and history indicate that the independent Canaanite city-states of Gen 15:19-21 are probably at least part of the 10 horns of the LBL. We see the descendants of those Canaanites as the Palestinians of today. Palestinians are being supported by, and are giving their support to the Moslem beast.

Luk 4:5-6 And the devil, taking him [*Jesus*] up into an high mountain, showed unto him all the kingdoms of the world in a moment of time. And the devil said unto him, All this power will I give thee, and the glory of them: for that is delivered unto me.

Since the Scarlet Beast transcends time, it would almost have to be a figurative representation of Satan's spiritual domain down through time. Satan was given dominion over all the kingdoms of the earth, so Satan's kingdom is probably the Scarlet Beast:

Rev 17:8 & 11 The beast that thou sawest was, and is not; and shall ascend out of the bottomless pit, and go into perdition: and they that dwell on the earth shall wonder, whose names were not written in the book of life from the foundation of the world, when they behold the beast that was, and is not, and yet is. And the beast that was, and is not, even he is the eighth, and is of the seven, and goeth into perdition.

There is something else peculiar about this satanic beast. This wicked beast "was, and is not, and shall ascend out of the bottomless pit." What can that mean? It means that before Jesus went to the cross, Satan had direct control over the empires of the world, but by John's time "he is not." Satan lost his dominion at that point, and was cast into the bottomless pit. So when and how was Satan cast into that pit, and by whom? Therein lies one of the most beautiful truths in the New Testament.

THE KINGDOM OF JESUS

In the sovereign plan of God, Jesus was not granted authority over all things, nor was He given a kingdom, until *after* He ascended to the right hand of God the Father. Before then, as a matter of biblical truth, the kingdoms of this earth were given into Satan's hand (Luk 4:6). But after the Lord was crucified, all things were given into Jesus' hands, and He now rules over a very real spiritual kingdom that exists today:

Eph 1:20-23 Which he wrought in Christ, when he raised him from the dead, and set *him* at his own right hand in the heavenly *places,* Far above all principality, and power, and might, and dominion, and every name that is named, not only in this world, but also in that which is to come: And hath put all *things* under his feet, and gave him *to be* the head over all *things* to the church.

That's reality. The kingdom of the Lord Jesus exists right now, today. Satan had it all his way until Jesus went to the cross. But after Jesus was crucified and rose from the dead, the enemy was finished, and he knew it. While Jesus was still on earth, He told his disciples about this several times:

Luk 10:18 & Joh 12:31 And he said unto them, I beheld Satan as lightning fall from heaven ... . Now is the judgment of this world: now shall the prince of this world be cast out.

Cast out to where? To the abyss. We find that same event recorded in Revelation but told to us in figurative language:

Rev 20:1-2 And I saw an angel [*Jesus*] come down from heaven, having the key of the bottomless pit and a great chain in his hand. And he laid hold on the dragon, that old serpent, which is the Devil, and Satan, and bound him a thousand years [*and thus, the thousand years of Rev 20 is a figure of the Christian Era*].[1]

You know, folks, we have been looking for Jesus' kingdom through the wrong end of our spiritual telescopes, and the Church has been fed "doctrines of demons." Just as Scripture declared three times, we Christians have been ruling with Christ since the cross.[2] We are even now "seated in the heavenlies with Him" (Eph 2:6). With all that has happened to the brethren during this era, it may not seem like we have done much ruling, but we have been ruling, all the same. Our kingdom is spiritual and it has never been of this world. It is in the heavenlies, where Christ is seated at the

---

[1] A full explanation of why Rev 20:1-7 should be viewed as a figurative picture of the Christian Era will be in Book II, if there is sufficient interest to publish it.

[2] 1Pe 2:9, Rev 1:6, Rev 5:10.

right hand of God. Christians are here on earth, among the servants of Satan, for a specific purpose:

> Mat 12:29 Or else how can one enter into a strong man's house, and spoil his goods, except he first bind the strong man? and then he will spoil his house.

Jesus bound the "strong man" at the cross and we are here to carry off Satan's goods by leading the lost to Jesus. Every time we lead a soul to the Lord, we are carting off Satan's property. So what do you think the enemy's response would be to saints who are despoiling his kingdom? Here is Satan's response:

> 2Ti 3:12 Yea, and all that will live godly in Christ Jesus shall suffer persecution.

We would like our Christian lives to be quiet and sweet and free from trials, but that has never been the Lord's plan for us. It wasn't true for the earlier saints of this era and it isn't true for us. Most who have gone before were tortured and murdered for their faith in Jesus. Is there some reason we should expect better? If we are not being persecuted, it is because we haven't done anything to deserve it. Being a Christian isn't some effortless little fire escape to keep us all from going to Hell. It is a lifetime commitment to our Lord and Savior, Jesus Christ, even unto torture and death. When a saint dies for Jesus' sake, it isn't a defeat, it's a victory, for "a servant is not greater than his Master":

> Rev 12:11 And they overcame him by the blood of the Lamb, and by the word of their testimony; and they loved not their lives unto the death.

That is what it is supposed to be like. Dead or alive, we reign with Christ. Satan was totally defeated at the cross, cast down, and throughout this era he has been bound in the abyss that he might not deceive the nations. But then we read ...

> Rev 17:8, 11 The beast that thou sawest was, and is not; and shall ascend out of the bottomless pit, and go into perdition ... and they shall wonder ... when they behold the beast that was, and is not, and yet is ... And the beast that was, and is

not, even he is the eighth, and is of the seven, and goeth into perdition.

Who was bound and cast into the bottomless pit (i.e., the abyss)? Satan, so Satan himself is the 8th Beast. He lost direct control of the nations at the cross, but he still "is," and he has been ordering his fallen angels throughout this age to tempt the hearts of men. The enemy didn't gain direct control of the nations again until 1967, after the 7th head (the Leopard-Bear-Lion) was fulfilled (Rev 12:12). Jesus bound Satan at the cross and cast him into the abyss, and to whom did He give the keys? The Lord gave the Church the keys:

> Mat 16:19 And I will give unto thee the keys of the kingdom of heaven: and whatsoever thou shalt bind on earth shall be bound in heaven: and whatsoever thou shalt loose on earth shall be loosed in heaven.

Defeat comes when we allow the enemy to lead us into the activities of his world to the point where we become indistinguishable from the unsaved. When he does so, we stop witnessing, and in a very real sense we loose Satan to influence the minds of those about us. In this generation of ease, the Church has gotten up off its knees – which loosed Satan's chains – and once again the enemy and his angels have been released upon the Earth (Rev 12:12). He is not a human antichrist, nor a talking statue on the old temple mount, and you are not going to visibly see him. But the enemy has been released from his prison, and he goes forth to deceive the nations:

> Rev 20:7-8 And when the thousand years are expired [*the Christian Era*], Satan shall be loosed out of his prison, And shall go out to deceive the nations which are in the four quarters of the earth, Gog and Magog, to gather them together to battle...

As this era draws to a close, you see national boundaries collapsing and a one-world super economy developing. A one-world religion is also appearing – a global ecumenism embracing many faiths. But that ecumenism is not the Gospel of Jesus Christ that is able to save men's souls from the wrath to come. It is the great religious whore, and it is inspired and run by the enemy.

THE TEN HORNS OF THE SCARLET BEAST

Within Israel's borders are the Palestinians, the Intifada, and the terrorist Hamas, while outside its borders lie a group of radical Islamic states. All are avowed enemies of God's people, and they fulfill the Leopard-Bear-Lion. But under the influence of the 8th beast (Satan), a godless council of ten is rising in the rest of the world for one hour (as time is reckoned in day-years that equals about two weeks).[1] With Satan loosed from his prison, he will again directly control the world's empires, but this time his kingdom will appear as ten political or economic regions.

> Rev 17:12-13 And the ten horns which thou sawest are ten kings, which have received no kingdom as yet; but receive power as kings one hour with the beast. These have one mind, and shall give their power and strength unto the beast.

In the past, visible world empires have always been controlled by visible public figures, but these ten horns are different. First, they don't come out of any of the heads but from the beast itself, so they are NOT the descendants of one of the seven previous empires. Second, they are not real kings or political leaders, but they receive power "as kings," so they are some kind of shadow empire operating behind the scenes, and that exactly fits global conditions today.

Folks, the following observations are not the fevered imagination of some conspiracy nut. These organizations do exist, and their influence on our land of liberty and their control of our financial systems can be read about in your own local paper. What's more, they exactly fit Bible prophecy about the final Gentile empire to come.

---

[1] In day=year time, one hour is 15.44 days, a little over two weeks.

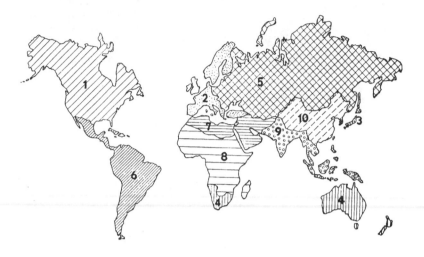

Map of the regionalization of the world system as proposed by the Club of Rome. This same map appears in many multi-national publications. However, Region 1 has now been modified to include Mexico, and that is what the implementation of NAFTA was really all about.

Shortly after World War II, at the suggestion of major European bankers, a group of financiers and politicians in the United States, formed the Council on Foreign Relations (CFR). That organization then founded the Trilateral Commission (TC). In 1954, the CFR hosted a meeting in the Bilderburg Hotel in Oosterbeek, Holland (thus the name, the Bilderburgers), with the express purpose of regionalizing Europe. Today's European Common Market is a product of that meeting. A further development of that meeting was the establishment of a European arm of the CFR named the Club of Rome. The Club was given one major task to perform: to divide the world into *ten* economic regions and plan for their unification under one economic head. If you noticed the number *ten* ... then alarm bells should start going off in your head. The Club held its first meeting in 1968, and proposed that these *ten* trading areas be known as *ten* kingdoms.[1]

---

[1] Nicolo Nicolov, *The World Conspiracy* (Portland OR, Nicolov 1974) p220.

Rev 17:12 And the ten horns which thou sawest are ten kings, which have received no kingdom as yet; but receive power as kings one hour with the beast.

The CFR and the Trilateralists see the world as *ten* kingdoms, and almost every important appointed or elected official in Washington, *of either party*, is a member of one or both of those organizations. The United States, Canada, and Mexico are Region One of this Ten-Horned hegemony, and that is what NAFTA was really all about: the forming of Region One.[1] These one-world organizations are all intertwined, with many members in common. There are other even less visible groups, like the Illuminati, but they all have a single goal: total economic, political and spiritual control of the world.

A few years later, the same international bankers and politicos put their plan into action by forming a committee called the General Agreement on Tariff and Trade (GATT). It should come as no surprise that GATT views the world as the same *ten* kingdoms envisioned by the Club of Rome. In speaking of these international financiers, Barry Goldwater wrote:

> The Council of Foreign Relations is the American branch of a society which originated in England...(and)...believes national boundaries should be obliterated and one-world rule established. The Trilateral Commission is international ... (and) ... intends to be the vehicle for multi-national consolidation of the commerce and banking interests by seizing control of the political government of the United States.

> What (they) truly intend is the creation of a world-wide economic power superior to the political government of the nation states involved. As managers and creators of the system, they will rule the future.[2]

---

[1] Gary H. Kah, *En Route to Global Occupation* (Lafayette, LA, Huntington House Publishers, 1992) pp.23-50.

[2] Barry Goldwater, *With No Apologies*, as cited by Nicolo Nicolov, *The World Conspiracy* (Portland OR, Nicolov 1974), pp161-164.

Goldwater's words were indeed prophetic. By 1987, the Trilateral Commission (TC) controlled 60% of the world's wealth through banks, presidents of multi-nationals, media moguls, politicians, and university authorities.[1]

The CFR has been in control of US policy for some time now. At the suggestion of the chairman of the CFR, President Nixon initiated a special enforcement arm of the executive branch known as the Federal Emergency Management Agency (FEMA). Ignoring both state boundaries and state governments, this agency sees the United States as *ten management regions* and recognizes the same *ten global kingdoms* as established by the CFR, TC, and GATT.[2] Structurally, FEMA behaves as a federal police force, answerable to the executive branch alone. From an organizational standpoint, FEMA and the BATF are not unlike the Gestapo or SS of Nazi Germany – they are totally independent enforcement agencies that are not answerable to congress. As a result, this country could be placed under martial law at the stroke of an executive pen.

Most of our important elected or appointed officials support a one-world government and the termination of the United States as a sovereign nation. Our handsome officials don't look like the betrayers of our Constitution because they wear coats and ties and sound oh so environmentally concerned and so "compassionate," but many are covertly maneuvering our country away from our traditional democratic form of government.

A small handful of honest legislators have tried to defeat the unconstitutional mandates being issued by one-world leaders through the executive branch and other authorities, but their efforts are not reported in the media (why am I not surprised), so the American people have no idea what is really going on. Those who do try to investigate the conspiracy, like Senator John Tower

---

[1] Hillarie du Berrier, *Bulletin* (Ft Collins, Co, Committee to Restore the Constitution, Dec 1989), p4.

[2] Mihajlo Mesarovic, *Mankind at the Turning Point* (New York, NY, E. P. Dutton & Co, 1974), p143

or Congressman Larry McDonald, are first discredited and then, by some mysterious fluke of fate, manage to get themselves killed in fatal airplane "accidents."

> Eze 22:27-28 Her princes in the midst thereof *are* like wolves ravening the prey, to shed blood, *and* to destroy souls, to get dishonest gain. And her prophets have daubed [*i.e., whitewashed over*] them with untempered mortar, seeing vanity, and divining lies unto them, saying, "Thus saith the Lord GOD, when the LORD hath not spoken."

Do not be deluded by what you hear on the nightly news, my friends. Major heads of most communications networks are also members of the CFR and TC and the "news" we hear from these sources is distorted to further one-world agendas. In its own publication, a CFR spokesman declared that it intended to make an end run around our national sovereignty to "get us to the new world order." The long range goal of the agencies controlled by international financiers is to bring us under a world financial government ruled by them.[1]

> Rev 13:17 no man might **buy or sell**, save he that had the mark, or the name of the beast, or the number of his name.

It all begins to fit together, doesn't it? But this would be of little importance to Christians who are walking in the Lord were it not for one cataclysmic problem. According to their plans, these *ten kingdoms* will be governed by a council of *ten*. These financial and political world leaders are not Christians. They are New-Agers, and many are outright occultists who are channeling with demons.[2] Most overtly hate fundamental Christians (no big

---

[1] Richard N. Gardner, Member of CFR, and former deputy Assistant Secretary of State for International Organizations under both Johnson and Kennedy. *Foreign Affairs,* the quarterly periodical of the Council on Foreign Relations (New York, NY April 1974), p52.

[2] There is a "meditation room" in the UN. In its center is a large block of black stone. Behind the stone is an abstract of what might be the sun or the all-seeing eye of Osiris. William Jasper writes in *Global Tyranny, Step by Step* (Appelton, WI, Western Islands): "New Age Guru Shri Chinmoy who leads meditations there says: 'The UN is a chosen messenger of God ... a divine messenger...One day the world will treasure the soul of the UN as its very own.'" Many one-world leaders are

164 *The False Prophet*

surprise, considering it is Satan who controls them), so when they come into power, persecution, imprisonment, and even death could again be the lot of the saints, just as the Bible predicts:

> Rev 11:7 And when they [*the Two Witnesses*] shall have finished their testimony, the beast that ascendeth out of the bottomless pit shall make war against them, and shall overcome them, and kill them.

Here is that beast out of the bottomless pit again, and the Jews and the visible church — the two Witnesses – are right in his gun sights. Now that we know who the ten horns are, the above verse exactly parallels the final prophecy about the harlot that sits on the Scarlet Beast:

> Rev 17:16 And the ten horns which thou sawest upon the beast, these shall hate the whore, and shall make her desolate and naked, and shall eat her flesh, and burn her with fire.[1]

As Christians play the harlot with the toys of the enemy, that woman, all decked out in royal apparel, who sits astride the beast, is none other than the visible church. She is the mainline Protestants, with their $25,000,000 sanctuaries, the Roman Catholics, with their papal authority, and all who have departed from the Word of God. The fate is sealed for the visible church. She is going to be destroyed, just like Revelation 11:7-8 foretells. Consequently, it is of inestimable importance for the "called out ones," the true Church, to know what it is supposed to do.

It isn't going to be life as usual ... going to church, raising our children and grandchildren, and saving for a retirement to some quiet nook in the country. Changing a few people in the Senate or Congress isn't going to make any difference. Getting a new President isn't going to change anything. Most of our revered political, industrial, and media leaders and many well known

---

New-Agers. Some are occultists while others are into eastern mystery religions.

[1] The term "whore" or "harlot" was used throughout the Old Testament to describe Israel when it turned away from the Lord: Isa 1:21, Jer 2:20, 3:1-8, Eze 16:1-41, Hos 2:5, etc. God hates it, and that same term is applicable to the Laodicean church of today.

religious names are members of the CFR, TC, COR, Illuminati, or all four.[1] Even if they weren't, they are trying to make peace with an Islam the Bible declares to be our last enemy.

A new, so-called "laughing revival" or some great charismatic experience won't change the outcome, either, because it won't change people's hearts. The magic show you see in the Church today is just another part of the enemy's grand deception – geared to lull Laodicean believers to sleep – and it has done just that. The truth is this: We are in the final generation, and Satan has been loosed upon the Earth:

> Rev 17:12-13 And the ten horns which thou sawest are ten kings, which have received no kingdom as yet; but receive power as kings one hour with the beast. These have one mind, and shall give their power and strength unto the beast.

These Ten Horns will give their power to Satan! Remembering the day=year calendar, an hour equals about two weeks. Those "hours" appear in Revelation seven times. The "hour of trial" of Rev 3:10 equals two weeks. "In that same hour" of Rev 11:13 equals two weeks. "The hour of judgment" of Rev 14:7 equals two weeks. "In one hour" is recorded three times in the destruction of Babylon (Rev 18:10, 17, 19). All of these are parallel prophecies about the same time, and because of these "hours," Armageddon will probably last about two weeks.[2] With today's weaponry, two weeks is probably long enough. If it were to last much longer, there might not be a Mount Zion upon which the Lord could stand when He returns.[3] The carnage could go on, but to save the few elect who are still hanging on by their fingernails, Jesus will put a stop to it.

---

[1] For additional information on one-world multinational agencies and their connection with the Masonic order: Gary H. Kah, *En Route to Global Occupation* (Lafayette LA, Huntington House, 1992).

[2] Pray that this hour is not a multiple because if it is, we could be looking at fifteen years of unimaginable trials.

[3] Mat 24:22 And except those days should be shortened, there should no flesh be saved: but for the elect's sake those days shall be shortened.

Rev 17:14 These shall make war with the Lamb, and the Lamb shall overcome them: for he is Lord of lords, and King of kings: and they that are with him *are* called, and chosen, and faithful.

Seven times in Revelation we read of the "hour of trial," and that hour is upon us. As of this writing, the Ten Horns are here, so with the exception of that hour and the battle of Armageddon itself, there is little prophecy left to be fulfilled.

Europe is fast sliding into the Middle Eastern camp with Islam the fastest-growing religion there. Amsterdam, Holland, home of the Anabaptist martyrs, has become a cesspool of iniquity. A witch in Zurich, Switzerland, knows only two Christians, and they don't live there. She met them in the train station, while they were touring Europe.[1] The USSR has collapsed, and there is credible evidence that her break-away states are selling nuclear arms to radical Islamic countries. As a result, Iraq, and possibly even Iran now possess nuclear arsenals and a covert delivery ability to get those weapons to any target they wish.

Rev 11:18 (*excerpts*) ... and thy wrath is come, and the time . . that thou shouldest destroy them which destroy the earth.

Amo 5:18-20 Woe unto you that desire the day of the LORD! to what end *is* it for you? the day of the LORD *is* darkness, and not light. As if a man did flee from a lion, and a bear met him; or went into the house, and leaned his hand on the wall, and a serpent bit him. *Shall* not the day of the LORD *be* darkness, and not light? even very dark, and no brightness in it?

The little flock that would give their all for Jesus knows by the Spirit that we have lost our beloved land. Greed has destroyed our crystal rivers and our endless forests. Our bountiful wildlife has been decimated, and the passenger pigeon is no more.

---

[1] The woman, dressed in all black, came up to a Christian family who was touring Europe and asked, "Where is your spiritual aura? You are the only people I have ever seen without a spiritual aura."

Woe to us, indeed. What are we to do? Well, in identifying the final enemies of the Church (the Leopard-Bear-Lion and Ten Horns of the Scarlet Beast), we are seeing the final signs that "our redemption draweth nigh" (Luk 21:28). But what we need to know is this: How does the Lord intend to hide us from the enemy's clutches.

A COUPLE MORE NEWS BRIEFS

www.IsraelNationalNews.com, Tuesday, Nov. 4, 2001

Two Israelis are dead, four are seriously wounded, and close to 40 others are hurt. These are the results of a Palestinian terrorist attack in Jerusalem this afternoon, in which one or more Arabs opened fire at a public bus near the French Hill junction. Alert citizens and soldiers opened fire and killed one terrorist, but not before he managed to fire several rounds of fire through the front of the bus - full with many high school girls returning from their studies. This was the 5th terrorist attack at this junction. One of the wounded is the driver, an Arab resident of eastern Jerusalem.

www.IsraelNationalNews.com, Tuesday, Nov. 6, 2001

How many more? Yet another Israeli civilian was murdered today when Palestinian terrorists ambushed his car with gunfire, south of Shechem. The terrorists were then overtaken and killed by an IDF force. It occurred not far from the Gilad Junction, named for Gilad Zar, who was murdered there in a similar attack about five months ago. The terrorist cell included members of Hamas, Fatah, and the Communist Party.

Wherefore, Come Out

Chapter 15

Wherefore come out from among them,
and be ye separate, saith the Lord,
and touch not the unclean thing;
and I will receive you,
And will be a Father unto you
and ye shall be my sons and daughters,
saith the Lord Almighty.

2Co 6:17-18

Though written over twenty years ago, the following allegory was never more appropriate than it is right now. It reflects Church conditions in the West as they exist today. I could have left this chapter out, but what good is a book that avoids truth just because it might make a few people uncomfortable?

THERE was a wicked city. In the middle of the city was a lofty church. That church had the tallest steeple that ever was built. In the steeple was the grandest bell that ever was made. When that bell was struck, it pealed forth with such a mighty knell that every building in the city rattled and some even shook to their foundations. It was all very frightening at first, because here and there a building had collapsed. But nothing had fallen in a long, long time, so the townsfolk had gone back to playing and dancing in the streets.

Seeing the church, Christian tried to go inside. But in the middle of the doorway was a massive iron gate. It had strong iron bars. Looking through the bars he saw lots of people inside. They were marching around in lock-step and chanting the same words to each other over and over and over again. They nodded approval to each other and kept telling each other how great they all were. They were God's elect, weren't they, and that was that.

Christian tried with all his might to open the gate, but it wouldn't budge. Then he noticed a heavy bronze plaque that was bolted to the gate with big bronze bolts. The headline engraved on the plaque read:

Church Doctrines and Traditions

Imposing and well-dressed men rode up in fancy cars. They mounted pedestals and stood guard over the plaque. The pedestals were very tall, and had signs on them that read, "Pastors and Evangelists Only". These elevated men held out collection plates and cried, "Give, give. Oh, give more! We need to build a bigger church and get a louder bell." Other men with arm-bands that read "Theologian" stood behind them as reinforcements.

People came up and bowed to the men, then they breathed on the plaque and polished it with their handkerchiefs, as you would a pair of glasses. Some folks even knelt before the plaque and kissed it. For all of them, the iron gate swung open by itself.

There wasn't any light on the plaque, the print was very small and there was an awful lot of it, so Christian held up his Bible (which shines in the dark) so that he could see. Squinting and adjusting his bifocals, he started reading the fine print. As he read, he muttered and groaned and became more and more agitated. Finally, Christian could stand it no longer.

"These doctrines do not agree with Scripture," he cried out in a troubled voice. Christian then opened his Bible and began to read it aloud. As each verse of Scripture was read, a crack appeared in the plaque, then another, and another, until the plaque shattered into a million pieces. As it splintered and fell, it made a tiny tinkling sound, but at that sound, the buildings of the wicked city quaked, and fell, until none were left.

The people in the church clapped their hands and giggled with glee, "The wicked city has fallen, the wicked city has fallen!"

They puffed out their chests and ran around shaking hands and congratulating each other. They never realized that it was not their bell, nor their lofty church, but the reading of the Bible that made the buildings fall. After the commotion had died down some, most of them went back to their marching, while others started working on a new plaque. They were so busy making sure that everyone was keeping in step that they forgot to take down their iron gate.

Christian didn't want to chant or march in lock-step behind an iron gate, so with Bible in hand, he turned and walked away. A few people with Bibles in their hands came out from the church and went with him. As they strolled along, they were all joyously singing, reading their Bibles, and sharing what they read with any passerby who would listen.

Soon there was a huge crowd around them singing and reading their Bibles. Then someone said, "Let's build a church and make a plaque ..."[1]

Now that was not an attack against good churches. If you are in one of the few good churches that remain in the land, *stay right where you are!* That is so important, I will say it again: If you are in one of the few good churches that remain in the land, you are most fortunate, *stay right where you are!* But it's not true for all. In many cities, spiritually hungry brethren spend Sunday after Sunday in a futile search for a Bible-teaching church, and can't find one.

Is this what your church is like? You go to services three times a week, seeking a little spiritual reality in your life, but in Sunday school they rehash last week's TV programs and talk about the

---

[1] The *Iron Gate* allegory does not appear in John Bunyan's *Pilgrim's Progress*, but to that elder brother goes the credit for the idea.

string of bass that George caught.[1] The pastor drones out some soothing old Charles Haddon Spurgeon sermon you heard twenty years ago, and you remember the last pastor, who ran off with that sexy-looking young organist. You also think about Tom, who lost his job and that his family didn't have enough to eat, but how that didn't stop the elders from giving the pastor a raise, nor from using the rest of the tithe to expand the sanctuary ... and you've been seriously asking yourself, "Is this what Jesus' church is supposed to be like, and is this really how God wants me to worship?"

You "sigh and groan" over the abominations committed in your midst, but what can you do? Your mother and father were life members of your church, you were baptized there, and the church down the street isn't any better. Could you even find a church that is truly concerned about your family's spiritual growth or that really has a heart to help you raise up your children in the nurture and admonition of the Lord?

If you are asking those questions of yourself and see no answers, then welcome to the true Church. The answer is the same as it has always been: It's in the person of Jesus Christ, and the Lord didn't make following Him difficult. He will show you through the Bible how easy it is to worship Him the way He intended for you to do it all along: "in spirit and in truth." It is all in God's Word, and we had better learn how, for very soon, the only refuge we may have left will be the Lord our God:

> 2Co 6:17-18 Wherefore come out from among them, and be ye separate, saith the Lord, and touch not the unclean thing; and I will receive you, And will be a Father unto you, and ye shall be my sons and daughters, saith the Lord Almighty.

It may not have happened to you yet, but if you can hardly stand what is happening to your church, or what is being taught

---

[1] 2Th 2:3 "Let no man deceive you by any means: for *that day shall not come,* except there come a falling away first."
2Ti 4:4 "And they shall turn away *their* ears from the truth, and shall be turned unto fables." So it is a falling away, not a great revival that will precede the return of Jesus.

there, sooner or later the Holy Spirit may lead you out of that church. With a heavy heart, many sound, Bible-believing Christians are now leaving established churches and attending no formal church at all. Some Christians are falling away, but a remnant – ah, the true Church – are forming little home groups. They are meeting in living rooms, cellars or garages, in any room large enough to hold a dozen brethren or so.

It's a scary thought, being on your own with just the Lord Jesus to sustain you. But don't worry, Jesus can handle it. He planned this whole thing long ago, and you are part of His plan. Just obey Him, and don't look upon what is happening as if it were a bad thing. It is the Lord's protection unto you. As we discussed in the last chapter, the visible church will soon be destroyed, and the Lord may be leading you out of it to hide you:

> Isa 26:20-27:1 Come, my people, enter thou into thy chambers, and shut thy doors about thee: hide thyself as it were for a little moment, until the indignation be overpast. For, behold, the LORD cometh out of his place to punish the inhabitants of the earth for their iniquity: the earth also shall disclose her blood, and shall no more cover her slain.

Five times in the New Testament we read about where the Church was located. In each case, the Church was in the home of an individual believer, and nowhere in the New Testament are we told that we should meet anywhere else.[1] In fact, the Greek word for church, ekklesia, could probably be better translated as "the called out ones," rather than "the assembly." The first century "called out ones" were unsung little groups of believers, meeting in homes where they were hidden by the Lord from the swords of their enemies.[2] Very soon, we, too, may have to assemble in the

---

[1] Act 8:3, Rom 16:5, 1Co 16:19, Col 4:15, Phil 1:2.

[2] The word "church" itself comes from the old English/Germanic word *kirke*, which meant a ritualistic pagan circle. Meeting in a *kirke* was rooted in the pagan concept that people could stand in a "circle of agreement," holding hands, to call upon demonic forces. (from *Church*, Smith's Bible Dictionary, Flemming-Ravell). Unaware of its true spiritual significance, many evangelical churches have now adopted this demonic ritual and have included it in their worship service. The

same way. The enemy hates the Church, and since he has now been loosed, he will soon physically attack it here in the United States, just like he is doing everywhere else on the planet.

Most of us have been programmed to believe that we can't worship the Lord, serve communion, baptize, or even have elders unless some sectarian seminary sends an "ordained" pastor to do the job in an "approved" manner: building a building complete with steeple, pipe organ, stained glass windows, a choir, a music minister, and so on. It just isn't so:

> Psa 51:17 The sacrifices of God are a broken spirit: a broken and a contrite heart, O God, thou wilt not despise.

> Joh 4:23 But the hour cometh, and now is, when the true worshippers shall worship the Father in spirit and in truth: for the Father seeketh such to worship him.

As church doors close, or as assemblies depart from the truth, the very survival of the true Church will depend upon the obscure godly sheep who are willing to walk before the Lord with contrite hearts, regardless of conditions around them. True saints will again need to learn from the Bible for themselves and gather with other like-minded brethren who are seeking the Lord's face. And it's all right to do that, you know. After all, the Lord ordained each of us to be a king and a priest:

> Rev 1:6 And hath made us kings and priests unto God and his Father; to him be glory and dominion for ever and ever.

We have a thousand pages of guidance on just how to gather together. It is called the Bible. Throughout the Christian Era various men and organizations have told us exactly what each verse was supposed to mean, or exactly how each church ordinance should be observed. But if we just trust Scripture, the Spirit of Truth, Himself, will teach us from it (Joh 16:13).

In this chapter, I considered writing the usual "rules" on how to hold a meeting, serve communion, baptize, and so on. But then,

---

Greek εκκλησία (Strong's No.G1577) ekklesia, ek-klay-see'-ah; from G1537 and G2564. *ek* meaning "out of," and *kaleho* meaning "to call" or "called."

I realized that I would be doing exactly what has gotten the Church into trouble all along: giving dictums of behavior beyond what Scripture already states. It's all in the Bible, folks. Everything the Lord wants a believer to do is in the Word of God. We simply need to follow His orders.

Suffice to say that the qualifications for eldership are found in 1Ti 3:1-7 and Tit 1:5-9, and how communion should be served is recorded in Mat 26:26-28 and 1Co 11:23-26. There is no scripturally specified method for baptism, but we do have early church history to guide us.

Many brethren in home churches now follow a first century church mode of baptism. First, they ask the new convert to renounce his past sinful life. Then they ask the convert to make a firm declaration of his new position in Christ Jesus. Though the words below are not struck in stone, the confession of faith goes something like this:

> *"I turn away from, reject, and totally renounce Satan, his kingdom, his angels and all his works. I repent of and renounce all my sins, and ask God to forgive me for them all. I accept the Lord Jesus Christ as my personal Savior and ask Him to become Lord of my life, Amen."*

Then, observing the command of Jesus in Matthew 28:19, the new brother or sister is baptized "In the name of the Father ... in the name of Jesus Christ His Son ... and in the Holy Spirit ... Amen." If the new believer is being immersed, he is immersed only once. But if he is being poured over, as was a first century practice, the convert is asked to kneel, and he is poured over three times: once as each name of God is spoken. But the mode of baptism is not nearly as important as getting it done.[1] Don't dawdle around.

---

[1] Southern Baptists would probably like me excommunicated for mentioning a mode of baptism other than immersion, however, pouring as an accepted mode of was clearly explained in the *Didache*, otherwise known as the "Teaching of the Apostles." Written in 85AD, the *Didache* is not an inspired work so it is not part of the Bible, but it does outline many practices of the 1st century church. William McGrath, *The Didache* (Christian Printing Mission, Minerva OH, 1976).

Baptism isn't just for show; it was given to believers for a sound spiritual reason (Act 22:16, 1Pe 3:21).

Brethren, unless I totally misunderstand Scripture, Christians and Jews will soon be persecuted in this land and we need to get ready for it. Not everyone in the church is saved. Many servants of the enemy are lurking there as wolves in sheep's clothing. They smile and sound sanctified, but if they don't really belong to Jesus, they would betray you in a minute.[1] You can't lead anybody to Jesus if you are lying face-down in some gutter with a bullet in the back of your head. Sound far-fetched? Well, it's a reality. That's the fate of Christians in many parts of the world, even as we write.

If you believe none of this could happen in your town or think that your friends and neighbors would never betray you, that is what the Protestant brethren in Ireland thought before 125,000 were tortured and killed by their neighbors. That is what 1,000,000 brethren in Cambodia thought before the Khmer Rouge wiped them out. That is what the Jews in Nazi Germany thought before they were herded into cattle cars that took them to the gas chambers of Buchenwald, Triblinka, and Auschwitz. And that is what we thought until the Twin Towers fell.

In Isaiah 26:20-27:1, the Lord directs us to hide at the end of time, and Jesus said, "Night cometh, when no man can work," Joh 9:4. Surely that time is upon us. So in accordance with those verses, it would be fitting to make preparations for a coming holocaust while we still have the freedom to do so.

To give you an idea of how persecution has already begun in Europe, the media in Holland are publicly calling our Christian brethren "dogs." Through this kind of overt anti-Christian prop-

---

[1] If you think that to be an overstatement: A deacon's wife in one of our local Baptist churches wore a red cape and tapped people on their forehead with a wand to drive out their demons. Laughable? That's a page right out of the occult, open witchcraft. In another case, a church elder and his wife were a young man's satanic godfather and godmother. In a third case, I personally know a Christian sister who, as a child, suffered years of unbelievable satanic ritual abuse at the hands of the elders of her "evangelical" church. This happened years ago, but she is still in hiding and fears for her life.

aganda, the Dutch people are being programmed to look favorably upon the havoc that may soon befall their little Christian community.

> Rev 18:4   And I heard another voice from heaven, saying, Come out of her, my people, that ye be not partakers of her sins, and that ye receive not of her plagues.

SO WHERE IS THIS PERSECUTION GOING TO COME FROM?

While it is true that the vast majority of Middle Eastern people are peace-loving, the religion they follow is not, as both history and current events so clearly show. Despite the good intentions of many Moslems, the Bible irrefutably identifies the Islamic states of Iraq, Iran and Syria and their associates as the final enemies of the church and Israel. As the Nigerian evangelist, M. Ali, clearly stated in his letter to me of October 19th, 2001:

> "You know as well as I, that Moslems the world over are pleased with the activities of Osama bin Laden. Never mind the duplicitous political statements of various Islamic leaders. They all see him as a twenty-first century Saladin. That America will destroy bin Laden's organization is not in doubt. The question is this: will it solve the hidden problem that *every radical Moslem is a potential Osama bin Laden?*"

As stated earlier, Islam would not be a problem if they had remained in the Middle and Far East as they had for the prior thirteen centuries. But fundamental Islam is spreading, not only in the Arab world, but in every place on earth where the Koran is taught. As a consequence, we are seeing these verses fulfilled right before our own eyes:

> Rev 16:12-14 (excerpts) And the sixth angel poured out his vial upon the great river Euphrates; and the water thereof was dried up, [thus unifying the Islamic world] that the way of the kings of the east might be prepared. And I saw three unclean spirits like frogs [the Leopard-Bear-Lion beast] come out of the mouth of the dragon, and out of the mouth of the beast, and out of the mouth of the false prophet. For they are the spirits of devils, working miracles, which go forth unto

the kings of the earth and of the whole world, to gather them to the battle of that great day of God Almighty.

Moderate Islamic governments supposedly support us while their fundamental mullahs stir up an ever-increasing unrest and hatred against all things Jewish or Christian. The Bible plainly foretells that Islam will be the final enemy of the Church and Israel, so a major future war against Islam is a certainty. This war in Afghanistan is not just a little minor conflict against a few extremists that we will be able to contain in Central Asia.

We can shout all we want that this is not a religious war, but to every fundamental Moslem in the Middle East, it is. Christian values that have been ingrained in our society for the last 2000 years stand against a Jihad mentality that is central to the Koran. Conflict is inevitable.

Last Trumpet

Chapter 16

When thou art in tribulation,
and all these things are come upon thee,
even in the latter days,
if thou turn to the LORD thy God,
and shalt be obedient unto His voice;
(For the LORD thy God is a merciful God)
He will not forsake thee, neither destroy thee,
nor forget the covenant of thy fathers
which He sware unto them..

DEU 4:30-31

But we are all going to be raptured out before the real bad times come, right? Let's make a little agreement between you, the Lord, and me. Let's take all our commentaries and set them aside for a while. Then let's take the Bible, and only the Bible, and see what it has to tell us about the final sequence of events.

Please be patient with me for making this a kind of nit-picking chapter. The I's are dotted and the T's are crossed because if the Scripture verses quoted below really mean what they say, then ALL of our current end-time ideas will need rethinking. Let's begin with a quote that is familiar to almost every Christian:

> 1Th 4:16-17 For the Lord himself shall descend from heaven with a shout, with the voice of the archangel, and with the trump of God: and the dead in Christ shall rise first: Then we which are alive and remain shall be caught up together with them in the clouds, to meet the Lord in the air: and so shall we ever be with the Lord.

All agree that those verses refer to the so-called "rapture" of the Church.[1] In fact, 1 Th 4:16-17 is one of the central passages in Scripture that supports the physical return of the Lord Jesus to this Earth. Note the WE. Paul was speaking to the Church of which he was part and we have every scriptural reason to believe that we also includes us. You and I and the rest of the church are the WE of 1 Th 4:16-17. That's relatively simple, isn't it?

Also note that Jesus is returning with the "trumpet of God." Now the Bible is full of trumpets, including seven in Revelation, so the next logical question is this: Which biblical trumpet is this one? Of all the trumpets in the Bible, at which one is the Church taken to be with the Lord?

> 1Co 15:51-52 Behold, I shew you a mystery; we shall not all sleep, but we shall all be changed, In a moment, in the twinkling of an eye, at the last trump: for the trumpet shall sound, and the dead shall be raised incorruptible, and we shall be changed.[2]

Ah, and there it is, the last trumpet! We are taken to be with the Lord at the last trumpet. That trumpet is singular, so no other trumpets are blown with it. Also, there are no modifiers such as, "except the trumpets of judgment," or "except the trumpets in Revelation." That needs to be emphasized:

There are NO exceptions! Not one Bible trumpet is left out!

---

[1] "Rapture" is in quotes because the author does not find the return of the Lord for the saints so characterized anywhere in Scripture. It is believed to have come from the Latin Vulgate's "raptao" in reference to this event. By definition, the word "rapture" seems more suitable for the mystery religions than it does for sober Christians looking forward to the most awesome event in all history, the return of Jesus. The whole "Rapture" concept may have been brought into the church by the publicists of Margaret Macdonald's vision. See Dave MacPherson, *The Rapture Plot*, (Simpsonville, SC, Millennium III)

[2] Compare this 1Co quote with the 1Th quote above it. In both, the dead in Christ are raised, and in both, trumpets are blown. Notice also that there are three more *we's*. Here is the point: If the *we* Paul was speaking of in 1Th 4:17 includes us, then so do the *we's* in 1Co 15:51-52. Believe it or not, there are those who claim that 1Th 4:16-17 is for the Church, while 1Co 15:52 is for the great tribulation saints. Nonsense! There are *we's* in both passages! Either both verses are for us, or neither are. We can't go arbitrarily picking through the *we's* in the Bible on the basis of some doctrine we wish to defend.

GRAPH NUMBER 20

The Last Trumpet

I Cor 15:51-52 Behold, I show you a mystery; We shall not all sleep, but we shall all be changed, In a moment, in the twinkling of an eye, at the last trump: for the trumpet shall sound, and the dead shall be raised incorruptible, and we shall be changed.

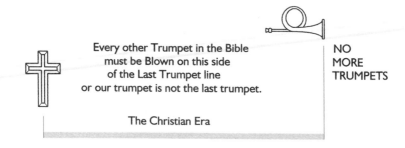

Every other Trumpet in the Bible
must be Blown on this side
of the Last Trumpet line
or our trumpet is not the last trumpet.

NO
MORE
TRUMPETS

The Christian Era

Note: The Last Trumpet draws a line in time. Every event predicted in the Bible must take place either to the right or left of that line. I Co 15:51-52 leaves no trumpets out, so that includes the trumpets in Revelation.

Recognizing that the church will be taken to be with the Lord at the one and only last trumpet of all time simplifies a doctrinal point the Church has been arguing about for over 100 years.

Mat 24:21 For then shall be great tribulation, such as was not since the beginning of the world to this time.

Mat 24:29 Immediately after the tribulation of those days ... the powers of the heavens shall be shaken:

Mat 24:31 And he shall send his angels with a great sound of a trumpet [a great trumpet, NASB], and they shall gather together his elect from the four winds, from one end of heaven to the other.

Note the sequence of events:

(1) Tribulation.
(2) After the tribulation.
(3) Great trumpet.

So isn't it obvious that the last trumpet comes after the tribulation?[1] Sure, and since the church is taken up at the last trumpet, the only way to defend the pre-trib rapture is to rewrite Scripture and put verse 31 before verse 21.[2]

No matter what our doctrines may have been in the past, the Bible states that our trumpet is the last, and the last trumpet does not blow until Rev 11:15, after the six other trumpets in Revelation have blown.[3] So the last trumpet is solid scriptural evidence that the Church will be on earth through the trumpets of Revelation. Now Brethren, that isn't just another irrational end-time theory. If we have ears to hear it, that is what the Word of God proclaims, straight out.

The last Bible trumpet blows in Rev 11:15, but the conditions surrounding that trumpet blast are described in chapter ten:

> Rev 10:6-7 ... that there should be time no longer: But in the days of the voice of the seventh angel, when he shall begin to sound, the mystery of God should be finished, as he hath declared to his servants the prophets.

What a tremendous verse. If there is a central Scripture about the chronology of the Lord's return, Rev 10:6-7 is it. As is true of every other creation of this present age, when the seventh trumpet

---

[1] Some believe the Church is "raptured" at the end of Rev 3 because "church" (the Greek word ἐκκλησία, usually rendered church), does not appear after Rev 3. Some logic. That's like saying Esther didn't believe in God because the word "God," does not appear in the book of Esther. But the main problems with their view are still the seven trumpets of Revelation chapters 9 - 11.

[2] Dave MacPherson writes, "Over the years I've privately contacted hundreds of the best-known evangelical scholars in regards to their prophetic views. The vast majority ... harmonizes 1 Thessalonians 4's coming with Matthew 24's coming, but the general public doesn't know this. If just a minority ... were to publicly reveal their positions, pretrib dispensationalism would receive a death blow." *The Rapture Plot* (Simpsonville, SC, Millennium III Publishers), p.233

[3] There are some denominational theologians who declare that this *last* trumpet does not include the seven trumpets in Revelation. Unbelievable as it may sound, they theorize that Revelation's seven trumpets are "special" trumpets of judgment excluded from the firm mandate of 1Co 15:52. There is absolutely *no* Scripture for their view, and it is counter to the plain testimony of the Bible: the declaration that we are taken to be with the Lord at the *last* trumpet!

sounds, it also appears that time itself will come to an end.[1] That's important, because understanding that time will come to an end affects our end time doctrine.[2]

The "mystery of God" is the Church in Christ Jesus.[3] So the Church as a betrothed body of believers on Earth will be concluded at this trumpet.

"As He hath declared to His servants the prophets." Which prophets is the Lord speaking of? We don't see any excluded, so these prophets are all the prophets in the Bible, both Old Testament and New. All prophecy will be fulfilled at this trumpet. Of course, this does not include those few verses which refer to the eternal Kingdom of God. That timeless state continues into infinity.

Let's look at the verse where that trumpet blast sounds. The 7th trumpet is blown right in the middle of Revelation, after the Seven Churches, after the Seven Seals, after six other trumpets, and after the Two Witnesses:

> Rev 11:15 And the seventh angel sounded; and there were great voices in heaven, saying, The kingdoms of this world are become the kingdoms of our Lord, and of his Christ; and he shall reign for ever and ever.

---

[1] The correct definition of the Gr. χρόνος (*chronos*) is "time," and it is so translated in the KJV. The modern translation of *chronos* as "delay" is probably invalid. Greek has several words for delay, including χρονίζω (*chronizo*) from the same root. If the Lord had intended delay, then He chose the wrong Greek word to express it. Though *chronos* appears 53 times in the NT, only in Rev 10:6 have modern translators taken the liberty of rendering *chronos* as delay. Strong defines χρόνος G5550, as a space of time, season, space, time, while. *Chronos* represents "delay" only by implication.

[2] If there is no more time after the 7th trumpet, there isn't any more time for another trumpet to blow. So our trumpet couldn't come after this 7th trumpet. Second, our trumpet can't come before this 7th trumpet either, or our trumpet would not be the last. So the 7th trumpet of Revelation is our last trumpet. It is the very trumpet at which we, the Church, are taken to be with the Lord!

Neither is the last trumpet going to sound over several years. The phrase "when he shall begin to sound" tells us so. At the very first peep out of that trumpet, there will be no more time! Time as a natural phenomenon will cease to exist, and we will be in the eternal Kingdom of God. This puts to rest the idea that the seventh trumpet could be blowing throughout a seven-year tribulation.

[3] Rom 16:25, Eph 1:9, 3:4, 3:9, 5:32, Col:1:27, 2:2.

The 7th angel sounds, and the Lord reigns forever. Right then, forever! After that trumpet blows, there won't be time for a tribulation, or for a 1000-year millennium. We will be going straight into the eternal Kingdom of God when that last trumpet sounds. Despite differing doctrines, that is the chronological picture as declared in the Bible.

GRAPH NUMBER 21

The Seventh Trumpet

Rev 10:6-7 ... that there should be time no longer: But in the days of the voice of the seventh angel, when he shall begin to sound, the mystery of God should be finished, as he hath declared to his servants the prophets.

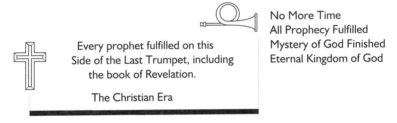

No More Time
All Prophecy Fulfilled
Mystery of God Finished
Eternal Kingdom of God

Every prophet fulfilled on this Side of the Last Trumpet, including the book of Revelation.

The Christian Era

Note: The Greek word translated "time" in Rev 10:6, KJV, is chronos (Strong's No. G5550, χρόνος. It appears that present-day translators have rendered chronos delay for doctrinal, rather than linguistic, reasons.

So when is the great tribulation? Matthew 24:21 tells us there was going to be one. Well, the Greek word for tribulation is thlipsis, also translated affliction and trouble. Thlipsis, used 37 times in the New Testament, almost always refers to the suffering of the saints. Here are a couple of very familiar verses:

Joh 16:33 These things I have spoken unto you, that in me ye might have peace. In the world ye shall have [thlipsis] tribulation: but be of good cheer; I have overcome the world.

Rom 12:12 Rejoicing in hope; patient in [thlipsis] tribulation; continuing instant in prayer.

2Th 1:4 So that we ourselves glory in you in the churches of
God for your patience and faith in all your persecutions and
[thlipsis] tribulations that ye endure.

Generally speaking, the unsaved don't go through thlipsis; they
are destined for orgy or thumos, God's wrath.[1] Orgy and thumos
are the two Greek words for wrath. So we saints will suffer
tribulation during the Christian Era, but we are not destined unto
a final wrath, but unto eternal salvation.[2] The wicked are destined
unto final wrath, the judgment of the Great White Throne, and the
second death. So when is "the great tribulation"? John tells us:

Rev 1:9 I John, who also am your brother, and companion in
tribulation, and in the kingdom and patience of Jesus Christ,
was in the isle that is called Patmos, for the word of God, and
for the testimony of Jesus Christ.

The tribulation of the saints began during John's time. May
God forgive us for forgetting the terrible suffering the saints of the
past have endured. Between two and twenty million Christians
were killed by the Roman Empire in tortures unimaginable. The
Catholic church killed up to twelve million more during the middle
ages. In our own generation alone, the Nazis murdered six million
Jews, and several million Christians. The Moslems have killed
millions as well. We don't read The Pilgrim Church, Fox's Book of
Martyrs, or Martyrs Mirror anymore, so we have lost our sense of
history. We have lost all memory of sufferings of our forefathers:

Mat 25:29 For unto every one that hath shall be given, and
he shall have abundance: but from him that hath not shall be
taken away even that which he hath.

The Lord has permitted the enemy to blind our eyes and we
have lost sight of God's big spiritual picture. The Great Tribulation
of the Church began with the stoning of Stephen, and continued

---

[1] Rom 9:22, Eph 5:6, 1Th 1:10, Rev 16:19.

[2] The "but unto salvation" of 1Th 5:9 is much beloved by pre-trib rapturists as
proof of their position. However, that phrase is not about a tribulation period at
all, but about the eternal salvation of the saints. The verse must be read carefully
if we are to grasp what it really teaches.

until the time of the Gentiles ended. From the Scriptures we have been looking at, it is obvious that all defined biblical times have been fulfilled in new Israel. As a result, the Great Tribulation is probably an epochal time that has been running throughout the Christian Era. In fact, since the true saints have suffered terribly ever since the cross, the "Great Tribulation" that Jesus spoke of may be His name for the Christian Era.

NEWS BRIEF

Arutz Sheva Israel National Radio, 11/12/2001, 1.09pm

Aaron Ussishkin, 50, the security officer of Moshav Kfar Hess, was shot dead by an Arab terrorist last night. He was alerted to the presence of a suspicious man at the entrance to the community, within pre-1967 Israel, about six kilometers northwest of PA-controlled Kalkilye and six kilometers northeast of Raanana. He ran to the site, and managed only to ask the Arab what he was doing there before the man shot him. Two other Israelis were wounded in the attack, and the murderer escaped.

Hour, Day, Month & Year
Chapter 17

To every thing there is a season.
A time to be born, and a time to die;
A time to kill, and a time to heal,
a time to keep silence, and a time to speak.

ECC 3:1-3 (EXCERPTS)

There are Seven Trumpets in Revelation and four different angels appear within the 6th Trumpet. Those angels can now be positively identified. Three of those angels have already been released and their messages were delivered between 688 and 1967!

> REV 9:13-16 And the sixth angel sounded, and I heard a voice from the four horns of the golden altar which is before God, one saying to the sixth angel who had the trumpet, "Release the four angels who are bound at the great river Euphrates." And the four angels, who had been prepared for the hour and day and month and year, were released, so that they might kill a third of mankind. And the number of the armies of the horsemen was two hundred million; I heard the number of them.

The Euphrates River area is the Middle East and the location of the Leopard-Bear-Lion. From other Scripture we recognize LBL to be the Islamic world! So these four angels were to be released from within the Islamic states.

That's not a whole lot to go on, so from what scriptures can we get further insight into these angels? Why, from somewhere between where this prophecy is given (Rev 9:14) and where the Lord sets up His eternal kingdom (Rev 11:15). These four angels appear after the 6th Trumpet blows, but before the Last Trumpet, (Rev 11:15). And since we go directly into the eternal Kingdom of God at the last trumpet ...

The only place to find out more about these angels would be between Rev 9:14 and Rev 11:14!

Now four angels don't appear between Rev 9:14 and Rev 11:14, but there is another clue to follow – TIME! Those four angels or messengers were prepared for four different time periods – an Hour, Day, Month, and Year. Guess what? The hour, day, and month each appear, once, in three different verses in Rev 11, all within the account of the Two Witnesses:

MONTH   Rev 11:2 "And leave out the court which is outside the temple, and do not measure it, for it has been given to the nations; and they will tread under foot the holy city for forty-two **months**.

DAY   Rev 11:3 "And I will grant authority to my two witnesses, and they will prophesy for twelve hundred and sixty **days**, clothed in sackcloth."

HOUR   Rev 11:13 And in that **hour** there was a great earthquake, and a tenth of the city fell; and seven thousand people were killed in the earthquake, and the rest were terrified and gave glory to the God of heaven.

The above is no coincidence. Those "month" and "day" angels were the Islamic scourge on the Holy Land from 688 to 1967. From context, it's obvious that the final "hour" angel is future, but where is the year angel?

Ἐνιαυτός (eniautos, Strong's No. G2094), usually translated year, does not appear between Rev 9:14 and Rev 11:14, but since all things are fulfilled by Rev 11:15, that "year" has to be in there somewhere. Let's examine the passage carefully to see if there are any other time designations that could be understood as "years."

REV 11:8-9 And their dead bodies will lie in the street of the great city which mystically is called Sodom and Egypt, where also their Lord was crucified. And those from the peoples and tribes and tongues and nations will look at their dead bodies for three and a half days, and will not permit their dead bodies to be laid in a tomb.

REV 11:11 And after the three and a half days the breath of life from God came into them, and they stood on their feet; and great fear fell upon those who were beholding them.

The Greek word (*hemera*), translated "days" in the above is ambiguous.[1] Since the above 3½ days are the only other time frame within the passage that could be possibly translated years, then maybe the correct translation for the above is years. Let's look at that possibility:

Rev 11:9 And those from the peoples and tribes and tongues and nations will look at their dead bodies for three and a half YEARS, and will not permit their dead bodies to be laid in a tomb.

Rev 11:11 And after the three and a half YEARS the breath of life from God came into them, and they stood on their feet; and great fear fell upon those who were beholding them.

We are in the New Testament era, using the Roman calendar, so if YEAR is the correct translation, using "I give you a day for a year" to interpret this prophecy, look at when we get to:

3.5 x 365.24 = 1278.34 Years
1967 (Jerusalem free) - 1278.34 = 688

The Dome of the Rock once again!

So the 3 ½ "days" of Rev 11:9-11 appear to be a repetitive prophecy about the Moslem domination of Jerusalem and the temple mount. If this is the correct way to view the passage, here is how the passage may be understood. To keep it simple, italic comments are inserted within the Bible text:

Rev 11:8-15, NASB (*Excerpts*) And their dead bodies (the empty churches) will lie in the street of the great city (Jerusalem) which mystically is called Sodom and Egypt, where also

---

[1] The Greek ημέρα (hemera, Strong's No. 2250g) found in vs. 9 and 11 is an ambiguous word, variously translated as day, moment, midday, time, and year, the correct translation depending upon context. In Rev 11:9 and 11:11 there are no contextual guidelines to determine the correct translation, so translators went with the most common usage, rendering *hemera* day. But twelve times, the translators of the NASB understood *hemera* to be year, Luk 1:7, 1:18, and 2:36 etc., so year is a perfectly acceptable translation.

their Lord was crucified. And those from the peoples and tribes and tongues and nations (*the Moslems in the surrounding lands*) will look at their dead bodies (*the empty churches*) for three and a half days (*Years of day=years, i.e., from 688AD to 1967AD*) and will not permit their dead bodies (the empty churches) to be laid in a tomb (*to be torn down*). And those who dwell on the earth will rejoice over them and make merry; and they will send gifts to one another, because these two prophets (*the Christians and the Jews*) tormented those who dwell on the earth (*it is torment for the lost when the gospel is preached and they do not repent*). And after the three and a half days (*after Jerusalem was freed*) the breath of life from God came into them, and they stood on their feet; (*After 1967, God's people returned to Jerusalem's churches and synagogues*) and great fear fell upon those (*the Palestinians and Moslems*) who were beholding them. And they heard a loud voice from heaven saying to them, "Come up here." (*Saints, both Jew and Gentile, taken to be with the Lord. Still in the future. Compare with REV 4:1*) And they went up into heaven in the cloud, and their enemies beheld them...and the rest were terrified and gave glory to the God of heaven. And the seventh angel sounded; (*the Last Trumpet*) and there arose loud voices in heaven, saying, "The kingdom of the world has become the kingdom of our Lord, and of His Christ; and He will reign forever and ever."

The above interpretation is in keeping with both Scripture and history. Now lets look at the 6th Trumpet (the 2nd Woe) again:

Rev 9:13-15 And the sixth angel sounded, and I heard a voice from the four horns of the golden altar which is before God, one saying to the sixth angel who had the trumpet, "Release the four angels who are bound at the great river Euphrates." And the four angels, who had been prepared for the **hour** and **day** and **month** and **year**, were released, so that they might kill a third of mankind.

Those four angels were released during the 6th Trumpet! From the prophecy of the Two Witnesses, we can see that three of those angels were freed from 688 to 1967. Remembering that "angel" really means messenger, look at what those messengers can now show us:

1. For **42 Months** Gentiles to dominated Jerusalem.
   A 1st "messenger" from the Middle East!
2. For **1260 Days** the Two Witnesses were driven out
   of the Holy Land.
   A 2nd "messenger" from the Middle East!
3. For 3 ½ *Hemera* (**Years**)the Lord permitted the Moslems to
   control Jerusalem.
   A 3rd "messenger" from the Middle East!
4. That **Hour**, the hour of trial, Armageddon.
   A 4th "messenger" from the Middle East!

Those angels were messages to the Church; and three of them have already been delivered to us, with malice, by the bloody swords of a fundamental Islam. But has the West been able to hear God's messengers from the Middle East, trumpeting to us down through the ages? It doesn't seem so, and it looks like the 4th messenger from the Middle-East, "the hour of trial," is just about to begin. Only a handful seem to notice, but this battle, too, will be fought against Islam. Fought by Israel and by what's left in the church who have ears to hear.

The above is separated by light-years from the prophetic superstitions of today's church, but few question our end-time traditions. If God were not in control, I would despair. Unless church leaders start doing their homework in the Bible instead of relying upon their dusty commentaries, I fear the church at large is doomed to remain in a spiritual darkness that will trigger the final holocaust. It's a tragedy too, because it doesn't have to be that way. But, as the Lord said through His prophets:

> Isa 5:13 ...My people go into exile for their lack of knowledge; And their honorable men are famished (for the Word of God), And their multitude is parched with (a spiritual) thirst.

> Hos 4:6 My people are destroyed for lack of knowledge.

A FINAL WORD

Within the Dome of the Rock is a large inscription in Arabic that reads: "God forbid that He should have a son." That and many other teachings of Muhammad have turned 1/5th of the world's population away from the Savior of mankind:

> " . . .The Christians call Christ the Son of God. That is a saying from their mouth. [*In this*] they but imitate what the unbelievers of old used to say. God's curse be upon them . ." (Surat at-taubah, 30).

So was Muhammad the false prophet of Revelation 16:13? Of course. This isn't just a little "clash of cultures" over the words of some minor figure in world history. It is God and His Word on one side and Satan and his lies on the other, in a war that began in the garden of Eden. The declarations of Muhammad stand directly against what the God of Heaven says in the Bible:

> John 3:36 &16 He that believeth on the Son hath everlasting life: and he that believeth not the Son shall not see life; but the wrath of God abideth on him ... For God so loved the world, that he gave his only begotten Son, that whosoever believeth in him should not perish, but have everlasting life.

Despite all claims to the contrary, during this Christian Era, all authority has been given into Jesus' hands!

> Phil 2:8-11 And being found in fashion as a man, he [Jesus] humbled himself, and became obedient unto death, even the death of the cross. Wherefore God also hath highly exalted him, and given him a name which is above every name: That at the name of Jesus every knee should bow, of things in heaven, and things in earth, and things under the earth; And that every tongue should confess that Jesus Christ is Lord, to the glory of God the Father.

Islam stands directly against those Bible truths. Understanding the Leopard-Bear-Lion beast as the Middle Eastern nations leads irrevocably to the conclusion that Islam and the fundamental Moslems are the final enemies of Almighty God. The day=year prophecies also show us that we are in the last generation of the

Christian Era. God knew the future of Islam and the Holy Land, right to the year, and God told us about it almost six hundred years before Muhammad was born.

There is nothing like those prophecies in the Koran. The Holy Land and Jerusalem again being under Jewish control is something Allah could not foresee. It is a fulfillment of Bible prophecy, not of Koranic prophecy. The comparison would be comic were it not so tragic. Many will stand before the Great White Throne in horror as their rejection of the truth is brought to a light from which they cannot flee. "It is a fearful thing to fall into the hands of the living God" (Heb 10:31).

There is one thought that should be repeated: Worldwide, there are about 1.2 billion people in Islam. Present estimates are that 10-15% of all Moslems are fundamental extremists. In other words, right now there are about 100 to 150 million people actively involved in the world's most dangerous splinter group and their numbers are rapidly increasing, particularly among the younger generation.

Now here's the point: Today there are an estimated three to five million Moslems in the United States. If that 10-15% statistic holds true for us, then from 300,000 to 750,000 of our American Moslems could be terrorist supporting Islamic fundamentalists. So are terrorists hiding in American mosques? The answer is obvious. If we don't root them out, our nation will never again be free of the threat of Islamic terrorism.

Not since the war of 1812 have enemy soldiers been allowed on United States soil. But liberal rhetoric and political correctness being what they are, we'll ignore God's warning about those who have rejected His Son. Instead, we'll march blithely on, to an Armageddon we'll be bringing upon ourselves.

FINIS

❦